BLUE GUIDE

THE BLACK SEA COAST

A GUIDE TO THE PONTIC PROVINCES OF TURKEY

PAOLA PUGSLEY

Somerset Books • London

THE BLACK SEA COAST
Updated and expanded chapter from *Blue Guide Turkey*

Published by Blue Guides Limited, a Somerset Books Company
Winchester House, Deane Gate Avenue, Taunton, Somerset TA1 2UH
www.blueguides.com
'Blue Guide' is a registered trademark.

ISBN 978-1-909079-81-5

Series editor: Annabel Barber
Town plans: Imre Bába © Blue Guides
Maps of Turkey: © Blue Guides
Prepared for press by Anikó Kuzmich.

Cover image: View of Sinop © Paola Pugsley

Acknowledgements
The author is grateful to Cambridge University Library
for providing unparalleled facilities.

www.blueguides.com

We welcome reader comments, questions and feedback:
editorial@blueguides.com

About the author

PAOLA PUGSLEY is a professional archaeologist with an interest in the Mediterranean and particularly in the eastern part of it. She first visited Turkey in 1970 as a tourist, driving all the way to the Nemrut Dağ, which she climbed on a most uncomfortable donkey. She vowed to return—but had to wait until the early 1990s. From then on she has worked every summer on excavations, moving steadily east. Her interest remains, as in her previous work with the Blue Guides (*Blue Guide Crete* and contributions to *Blue Guide Greece the Mainland*), in bringing to life the visible and invisible past and in encouraging visitors and armchair travellers alike to engage in and see the sites both in their long-term development and physical setting.

CONTENTS

THE GUIDE

PRACTICAL INFORMATION

MAPS

Introduction

'There's not a sea the passenger e'er pukes in
Turns up more dangerous breakers than the Euxine.'

When Byron penned this two-liner in his *Don Juan* (*5, 5*) he may have been more interested in finding a rhyme for Euxine than maligning the body of water that he praised elsewhere as the 'noble sea'. That said, he was not the only one to comment unfavourably upon it. Before him the seasoned 17th-century traveller Evliya Çelebi had vowed never to set out on those treacherous waters again; after a disastrous crossing he had been shipwrecked on the coast of Bulgaria, where he spent eight months recuperating in a Dervish *tekke*. He used his time wisely though, completing ten recitations of the complete Koran, so bringing his personal best to 1,060.

'Euxine' is the Greek name for the sea: *Euxinos Pontos*. The Turks call it Kara Deniz, which translates exactly as 'Black Sea'.

WHAT'S IN A NAME: THE CASE OF THE BLACK SEA

These days the body of water bordered by southern Russia, the Balkans, Anatolia and Georgia is called the Black Sea (Kara Deniz). The name seems to be Turkic in origin, so it could date to the 12th–13th century. Other nations around the sea have since translated its name into their own languages. But why 'black'? First, there is probably an intended contrast with the Mediterranean, which the Turks call the 'White Sea' (Akdeniz), very likely because of its blinding glare as the strong light is reflected upon the water. Nothing of the sort on the Black Sea: here all speaks of mists, darkness and silence. So it is not surprising that the Turkic nomads, as they peered from the heights of the plateau or ventured to the winter pastures by the shore, called the body of water 'black'. Moreover, it might also have looked dark in comparison to their own sunnier steppes. Alternatively, another explanation is that any metallic object submerged 100m or so in the Black Sea waters, as any local fisherman will tell you, turns black.

It was not always the Black Sea. Strabo (1st century AD) called it Pontos, which supposedly means 'The Sea': the sea *par excellence*, as viewed from Amasya, slightly inland, where he was born. Apparently though, *'pontos'* does not only have a Greek etymology; the word is present in local languages from Thrace to Armenia where it means a bridge, a way or a ford, just like the Latin *'pons'*. The emphasis is no longer on a 'sea' but on a 'bridge' between Asia and

Europe. To confuse matters further the dichotomy inhospitable/hospitable (*axinos/euxinos*) has been around since the 5th century BC when the Greek poet Pindar used it in one of its odes. By then the Black Sea had been tamed by the Greek colonists; it was no longer inhospitable. Euxinos Pontos remained the official denomination until the Euxine became an Ottoman lake in the 15th century.

And finally, the sea is 'anoxic', which is an epithet rather than a name. The Black Sea is dead: or at least, some 200m below the surface it is. A combination of a large inflow of fresh water from the discharging rivers, poor ventilation, low evaporation and limited aeration have killed life in the depths: there is no oxygen there. The vast amount of organic matter brought in by the rivers is broken down by bacteria that do not use oxygen: what is not broken down, accumulates. The whole mass is saturated with a hydrogen and sulphur compound (the one that turns metal black). The sediments, 8 to 16km thick, remain to this day unexplored.

But this guide is not about the Black Sea itself; it is about its southern coast, now more readily accessible by air or by road than by water: braving the sea is no longer a requirement as was the case in the past. The guide starts in the very east, where present-day Turkey meets Georgia; it then moves steadily west inland over the Pontic Alps to cover Erzurum, Sivas and Tokat—which are certainly not Pontic cities, though they had strong commercial ties with the coast. Trabzon, its hinterland the Matzouka Valley, and the ancient Chaldia region are given a separate section as it is difficult to disentangle Trabzon from its immediate surroundings. The cut-off point at ancient *Heracleia Pontica* is to an extent arbitrary. Paphlagonia, with its rugged mountains and wild inhabitants (wild, that is, in the past), ends here and the area to the west, the ancient Bithynia, has always been very much in the sphere of influence of the City (be it Constantinople, Byzantium or Istanbul). From that point the narrative runs along the coast all the way back east.

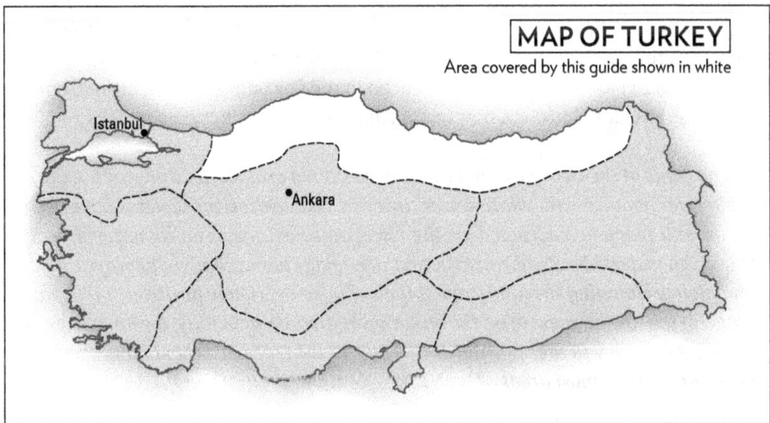

Ardanuç, the Georgian Churches & Lake Çıldır

By a fluke of historical development this region, in the hinterland of Hopa (*map D, 1*), was the only part of the Kingdom of Georgia not in Arab hands in the 9th–10th centuries. Ardanuç was its capital and the land was known then as Tao-Klardjeti, or 'Upper Iberia', the Classical name for Georgia. Steep, severe and mountainous, it was the ideal stronghold from which to fend off the Byzantines on the narrow coastal plain to the west and north and the Armenians to the south. Originally the region had been in Armenian hands, but when they came into conflict with the Arabs, King Ashot the Great of Georgia moved in to set up an independent kingdom in 820, leaving Tbilisi to the Caliph of Baghdad. Apart from defence, the area also had strong commercial potential. Ardanuç was on a trade route leading from the Black Sea north to Georgia, south to Armenia and beyond to Persia.

Trading and peace had the desired effect. Money flowed in, Christianity expanded under the influence of Gregory of Khandzta, busy founding monasteries and copying manuscripts; rulers and notables contributed generously to the cause. But it was short-lived. The last king, David the Great, had no children and the precious peace was lost in a succession of intestine squabbles and the incursions of the ubiquitous Turkmen. Then the Arabs moved out of Tbilisi after a 400-year rule; Georgia enjoyed a resurgence, with the king now ruling from Tbilisi. As a result, the political and commercial centre of the area shifted north; the district of Tao-Klardjeti became peripheral and in fact was never heard of again. It is said that there were Georgian speakers in the valleys up until the 1970s; there are probably none now, but vestiges of the Georgian past can still be experienced in the few buildings that have survived, notably the ancient churches, now in varying states of dereliction and decay.

NB: The ruins of the Georgian churches are scattered around the valley of the Çoruh, a rapid river popular with white-water rafters. Great hydroelectric dams have been—and are still being—constructed on the river, and the impact on its natural beauty has been considerable. Road construction involving tunnels and motorways on stilts is completely changing the landscape. Much of it, sadly, is now positively ugly, partly because of the raw newness of all the building. With time, hopefully, the landscape will improve, though it will take a while as this part of the Black Sea coast is harsher, drier and less green than most areas.

ARDANUÇ & THE GEORGIAN CHURCHES

Ardanuç (*map D, 1*) is a quiet little town, seldom sought out by tourists, but it works as a base from which to visit some of the Georgian churches. It also has by far the best castle in the area—and it has not yet been restored, which makes it all the more atmospheric. Perched on a tall rock looming large over the old capital, **Ardanuç Kale** cuts an impressive figure. It is signposted at the entrance of town; the road is quite reasonable and runs all the way round. The last stretch, though, must be done on foot: there is no set route to negotiate the tall, bare cliffs. The core of the building is said to be Armenian but the visible remains are of the 9th–11th centuries. Still apparent among the ruins are the defensive walls, remains of the old town, a cistern and the round apsed chapel dedicated to SS Peter and Paul, built in large, expensive sandstone ashlars.

Northwest of Ardanuç is the Cehennem Deresi Kanyonu, or **'Hell's Canyon'**, a steep rocky gorge down which flows the tumbling river. In its upper reaches it opens out and offers lush green banks. Sadly, at the time of writing, garbage tippers had been at work.

CHURCHES OF THE DISTRICT

According to Chris Hellier, who has conducted an architectural study of the surviving churches, there were originally around 80 of them. Most are now lost and those that survive need more than just an explanatory panel to save them from utter ruin. Their crumbling structures need serious, sustained attention and a thorough recording programme would help greatly.

Stylistically the churches can be divided into two groups: the early 7th-century type with a quatrefoil plan within a circle (not dissimilar to the contemporary Armenian cathedral at Zvarnots) and the basilica, in its simple form or later, with a more complex cruciform plan. The churches listed below conform to this latter type. Of the former, circular type, the finest example was the church at Bana, almost completely destroyed in the Russo-Turkish wars of the 19th century.

DOLİŞHANE & YENİ RABAT

West of Ardanuç at **Dolişhane** (Hamamlı; *map D, 1*), a 10th-century Georgian church beckons c. 3km off Route 010. It was a mosque for a time after the 17th century when the dome was rebuilt; later in the mid-20th century, when a new mosque was erected nearby, it was abandoned and used as stables. Its main attraction are its few surviving ornate windows.

South of Ardanuç on a secondary road to Ardahan, is the Georgian church of **Yeni Rabat** (*map D, 1*), dated very tentatively to the mid-11th-century. Also known as Schatberdi Manastiri, it sits in a walnut grove. It has suffered extensively from stone robbing, but the beautifully ornate windows have survived because they are high up. The fine manuscripts for which it was famous are in Tbilisi.

BAĞBAŞI (HAHO) & ÖŞK VANK

Heading south from Yusufeli on Route 950, along the valley of the Tortum Çayı, a fine river with beautiful waterfalls, the first stop is Haho, now **Bağbaşı** (*map D, 3*), for a monastery complex. The church, a 10th-century building dedicated to the Mother of God, was converted into a mosque in the 18th century. It is variously known as Taş Camii or Meryem Ana Kilisesi. It is in a reasonable state of repair (the dome has been rebuilt and there is a roof) but is normally closed apart from at prayer time on Fridays. The entrance is at the south end with blind arcades. The only way to catch a glimpse of the interior is to peer though the apse window near the chimney flue connected to the stove inside. It must be perishingly cold in winter. The nearby chapel is full to the ceiling with logs. At the west end, the refectory and scriptorium are later additions. Nothing remains of the other buildings (chapels and monastery). The famous Hahuli Triptych, with its enamelled icon of the Mother of God, is now in Tbilisi.

The **Monastery of Vank** (Öşk Vank) is a little further on along the river to the left before the artificial lake (Tortum Gölü), well marked on a road to Çamlıyamaç. It sits in the green at the top end of a broad valley. A mid-10th-century foundation, it retained its importance as a cultural and religious centre well into the 15th century. It was converted into a mosque towards the end of the 19th century and functioned as such until 1980. Of the frescoes commissioned by Patriarch Gacik in 1036, only a few biblical scenes can be seen in the apse. The cruciform dome construction in ashlar blocks has a Gothic feeling, especially when viewed from the inside, where the lofty vertical lines are not interrupted by porches. On the outside, note the delicate carvings of the window frames and the worn figure of the donor in luxurious robes carrying a model of the church.

İŞHAN & DÖRT KİLİSE

At **İşhan** on Route 060 (*map D, 1*), the church looks exceedingly pretty in its verdant setting with a backdrop of tall mountains. This was originally a monastery. The church and chapel are the only parts surviving. It is said to have been founded by Saba, a nephew and follower of Gregory of Khandzta, on the site of an earlier Armenian church. The main body of the present edifice is mid-11th century with 12th–14th-century additions. Used as a cathedral until the 17th century, it housed the headquarters of the Ottoman officers at the time of the war against the Russians. It was then a mosque until 1983. Now it is on the list of national cultural monuments. This has not helped it to keep its roof on, though the tall dome supported by massive piers is still standing. The cruciform structure has a unique arrangement at the end of the eastern cross arm, with an impressive horseshoe-shaped colonnade. Of the fresco decoration, only the scenes in the cupola with the '*Ascension of the Cross*' have survived in good shape. The façade, in well-cut multicoloured stones, has blind arcades, a pattern which is repeated on the exterior of the dome. The chapel southwest of the cathedral, a single-nave structure, is also dedicated to the Mother of God, according to the inscription. Of the prolific painted decoration only the scene in the apse with the enthroned Christ can be identified.

Dört Kilise is off the Çoruh river, going north into a side valley at the village of

Tekkale, on Route 050 from İspir. The building was completed by the end of the 1st millennium. It is a simple, imposing basilica of harmonious proportions, well in tune with the peaceful setting. The exterior is decorated with blind arches. In the semicircular apse, faded frescoes show *Christ in Majesty* and the *Virgin Enthroned.* To the west of the church are remains of the scriptorium and refectory.

TBETİ CATHEDRAL

To the northeast of Artvin on the way to Lake Çıldır, the Georgian Cathedral of Tbeti, an early 10th-century ashlar construction of imposing proportions, was the seat of a bishopric. In its present overgrown state (the dome collapsed in 1953 at a time when it was no longer used as a mosque) it is quite difficult to make out its plan, but there is clearly local interest in making something out of what is left, at least judging by the two tea houses that have opened nearby to cater for the rare tourist. The stonework and the delicate carvings around the windows are impressive. To find it, take the narrow road signed to Veliköy at Şavşat Kale (north off Route 010), continue to Cevizli and take a turn marked Zigaoğlu. On the way, note some typical wooden houses built like Russian *isbas,* with horizontal notched logs.

LAKE ÇILDIR

At Lake Çıldır (*map D, 2*), one is still in the historical Tao-Klardjeti district but much higher up. The lake is at 1900m and is overlooked from the west by the Kısır Dağ and the Akbaba Dağ in the east, both over 3000m. There are some Georgian churches around the lake, now turned into mosques. They remain difficult to date but the poor quality of the workmanship suggests that they might have been built later, when the region was still Georgian but the centre of power had shifted north to Tbilisi. They could be the work of some local wealthy family.

The lake itself was part of a larger watery expanse in geological times, when it was contiguous with Lake Aktaş to the north (on the border, now equally shared with Georgia), until cut off from it by a thick lava flow in a massive eruption. Lake Çıldır is large, not very deep but full of fish, which attract hosts of storks in spring when they arrive from Africa, and again at the end of the summer when they prepare to migrate.

After taking your fill of birdwatching, head for the town of Çıldır to the north and further into the valley towards Yıldırım and beyond to **Şeytan Kalesi** (the Devil's Castle), perched on a ridge projecting into the Kara Su. The present structure, incorporating medieval elements, is Ottoman though it has had a recent facelift. It includes a tapering keep, a first ring of walls, a lower platform and an outer bailey, and is set against a breathtaking backdrop of tall cliffs.

PRACTICAL TIPS

GETTING THERE

Public transport is erratic in this part of Turkey and heavy vehicles involved in the hydroelectric dam construction on the Çoruh can cause serious delays. If you plan to visit the Georgian churches, it is much easier if you have your own hire car, or hire a taxi locally. The main centres are served by buses and local *dolmuş*. Artvin and Hopa are linked to Trabzon by bus (journey time 4–5hrs). From the Artvin *otogar* (about half a kilometre from the centre) there are buses to Ardanuç.

WHERE TO STAY AND EAT

The area is not devoid of accommodation. **Borçka** (*map D, 1*) has places to stay because of the dam programme on the Çoruh river. The grandly named Grand Baraj Otel (*T: 466 415 4343*) is anything but grand but it is fine for a night. The town shuts down early: be sure to secure a meal before 8pm. **Artvin** (*map D, 1*) offers more choice. Reaching the town involves a challenging drive to the top of the cliff, but when you get there, the Mersivan Hotel (*T: 466 212 3333*) is inexpensive and welcoming. There is a choice of eating places and there is even a shop where you can buy *pekmez* and Xenophon's 'mad honey' (*see p. 95*). Ask for *'deli bal'*: it has a very distinctive taste. In **Ardanuç** there is a single hotel, the Ürün Otel (*T: 466 611 4206*), which is acceptable and inexpensive. It is situated north of town in the outskirts (which is not particularly convenient), on the road from Artvin.

FESTIVALS AND EVENTS

If you are in the Artvin area in July, inquire about the *Kafkasör Festivalı,* where the dispersed rural communities come together for various events including the *Boğa Güreşi* (a sort of corrida with two bulls and no matador).

Trabzon

The queen of the Black Sea, the capital of the ancient province of Chaldia and the ante-chamber to central Asia, Trabzon (*map C, 2*) has now settled down to being a provincial capital. The glittering days of the Empire and the commercial boom of the 19th century are over. Nor has modern development been kind to it. The decision to reclaim land on the shoreline and the relentless road-building programme to ease the east–west traffic have erased much of the physical remains of the past, but not completely. The place is certainly worth a couple of days exploring, to see Aya Sofya (don't plan to go there on a Friday) and to get a feel for the old town between the citadel and the harbour, along Uzun Sk and Maras Cd. Trabzon is also a place bristling with shops. A visit to the busy market can be a lot of fun and a way to find out what the latest novelty is. In 2014 it was tea glasses with the Sultan's monogram (*tuğra*) in gold.

THE HISTORY AND THE PEOPLE

It all started on a flat rock overlooking the sea and protected on either side by deep ravines. This was the nucleus of the original settlement: Greek colonists from Sinop expanding east in a land that was certainly not empty (*see below*). The aim was to trade with the people inland, the Mossynoeci (Xenophon: *Anabasis, 5.5.10*). The flat rock, which features on some coins, had the shape of a table, hence the name *Trapezous*, the Greek for 'table'. The town's name has varied over the centuries: Trapezous, Trebizond, Trebisonda, Trapezunte, Tarabzundah, Ťrap'uzani; here the latest version, 'Trabzon', will be consistently used.

Trabzon remained more or less insignificant until Rome began expanding east. In AD 62 it became the supply harbour for Corbulus' Armenian expedition. Trabzon's natural harbour facilities have never been exceptional, but when the fortress of Satala (*see p. 35*) was built in AD 75 as part of a strategic frontier line stretching from *Melitene* (today's Malatya) to Samosata and beyond, it became an all-important supply point. Coastal roads were then non-existent and inland traffic was difficult. Up until very recently, Trabzon has been connected to Istanbul and the rest of the world by sea. But with the Romans Trabzon acquired its first proper road inland, remains of which have been identified around the Zigana Pass. It also acquired its first inscriptions: military and in Latin.

THE LURE OF THE BLACK SEA: THE GREEKS

The archaeology of the Greek colonisation of the shores of the Black Sea remains to be carried out, especially on the south coast. Our information today comes largely from the written sources. The beginning of the phenomenon can be tentatively placed in the 7th century BC, making it later than the Greek colonies on the west coast of Anatolia, the Greek Ionia, and contemporary with the sparse Greek presence on the south coast facing the Mediterranean.

Ancient authors maintain that the main cause was the usual lack of land (stenochoria), the same problem that drove the Greeks to Italy and to the east coast of the Aegean. There is also the conundrum of the famous 'Catalogue of Ships' in the *Iliad* (2.851–7) which would suggest that by the 8th century BC (i.e. the time of Homer) there was some knowledge of the western seaboard of the Black Sea up the Halys River (to add to the adventures of the Argonauts, which at that time would have circulated orally), unless of course it is a later interpolation. What is certainly known is that by the time Xenophon was making his way back from Mesopotamia, there was a string of Greek cities on the coast and he more or less relied on them to get him and his men home. Whether each settlement had an ethnically distinct background is not clear. Excavations of Greek colonies (e.g. *Pithecusae*, now Ischia, in the Bay of Naples) show that colonies could be quite a mix ethnically. The oldest is *Sinope* (modern Sinop), presumably because of its double harbour, its seclusion from the hinterland and its proximity to the northern shore, where the Greeks also had colonial interests. Traditionally there was a total of 96 colonies around the Black Sea: coastal emporia, not contiguous, but separate concerns, with harbour facilities and little hinterland. They must have relied for their survival on good relations with the local tribes; indeed, as they set themselves up as proper cities, they paid protection money to the native chieftains. It was essential to do this in order not to be overwhelmed and also to access the commodities they wanted to trade: textiles, hides, wood, metal, slaves, pigments and wax, as well as fish, oil, grain, honey and salt.

Information about the relations with the indigenous inhabitants is scanty. Recent finds of 6th-century Greek pottery deep inland, including Greek-style architectural tiles and terracottas with Greek motifs in a native context, suggest a more sustained interaction, but present evidence is not sufficient to allow any conclusions to be drawn. The Greek presence on the Black Sea coast, and subsequently in its hinterland, has a long history. It may well have started earlier than the colonies, as specimens of Greek pottery dated 1200–800 BC and found deep into the Halys basin suggest. But how strong was the continuity over a period of over 2,000 years? How justified were the Pontic Greeks (*see p. 27*) of the 19th century in claiming a Greek heritage? Certainly by the time the Greeks of the Black Sea were forcibly returned to the 'motherland', Greece was an alien country to them.

Hadrian made Trabzon the base of the *Classis Pontica* (the Pontic fleet) in AD 124 and built harbour structures to the north of the citadel. The town expanded to the east around the *agora*, located in today's Meydan and connected to the citadel along two main thoroughfares, Maraş Cd and Uzun Sk. The city was unwalled. Not much remains of Roman Trabzon. The marauding Goths and successive invaders took their toll from the mid-3rd century, but most was lost to Comneni redevelopment of the 13th–14th centuries, when a certain amount of Classical material was reused, as was the case with the monumental inscription to Hadrian that now forms the lintel over the north door of the Church of the Panaghia Chrysocephalos. Under the emperor Justinian in the 6th century, Trabzon received some attention from Byzantium as an important settlement on a difficult border, the last bulwark against Persia. However, as time progressed and enemies multiplied, it became clear to the Trapezuntines that they would have to look after themselves. The capital was just too far away. This they did to an impressive degree in 1204 (*see below*), meanwhile maintaining a strong commercial bias. As the Muslim geographer Ibn Hawqal, who died at the end of the 10th century, reports, *Tarabzundah* was the meeting place for Byzantine, Armenian and Muslim traders, who came together in annual fairs to trade all manner of textiles, spices, furs, skins and slaves.

THE EMPIRE OF TREBIZOND

Things took a dramatic turn in 1204 when the crusaders sacked Byzantium and turned it into the capital of their new Latin Empire. The Byzantine Empire was forced eastwards and reinvented itself on the Asiatic shore of Bosphorus, under the name of the Empire of Nicaea. In the east were two men who saw themselves as the rightful heirs of the throne of Byzantium: David and Alexios Comnenos, whose grandfather had been ousted by the usurping Angelos dynasty, which in turn had fallen to the Latin crusaders. Now they felt the time was ripe for action, especially as they could count on the assistance of their aunt, the Georgian Queen Tamara, with whom they were staying in Tbilisi. The Empire of Trebizond was born. It was intended originally to stretch quite a way west. The Comneni had estates in Paphlagonia, in the Kastamonou region, but that piece of coast was soon lost—not to the Byzantines but to the nomadic Cepni Turkmen, who relentlessly infiltrated from the west and south to gain access to the lush winter pastures by the shore, and to the Seljuks, who were looking for an outlet to the sea. Sinop was in their hands by 1214 and over time the coast became dotted with Turkmen emirates, with whom the Comneni coexisted thanks to some delicate diplomatic footwork (*see 'Trapezuntine Princesses' below*)

The core of the Trebizond Empire was not large but it was compact and homogeneous. While the deep hinterland down the south slopes of the Pontic Alps had always been in the hands of local warlords, who now cast in their lot with the Comneni, the Matzouka Valley, cut by the *Pyxites* (now respectively the Maçka Valley and Değirmen Dere), immediately to the south of Trabzon up to the Zigana Pass, was solidly Greek—and so it remained to the bitter end. There were 38,000 Greeks there in 1914 in 70 villages, of which 47 were pure Greek, 14 Turkish and 9 mixed.

TRAPEZUNTINE PRINCESSES

For the Grand Comneni, as the Christian emperors of Trebizond styled themselves, diplomacy was probably the best way to survive in a hostile environment. Enemies were present on all sides, and they were all Muslim. If you could not fight and crush them, it was probably more prudent to join them and hope to fend off the evil day, buy time: it was a strategy of survival. And for this purpose, the Comneni used the best commodity they had.

Trapezuntine princesses enjoyed a high reputation for beauty, refinement, learning and class. They were highly prized by non-Christians, mainly as an exotic addition to the harem. Between the mid-14th and mid-15th centuries, a number of daughters of the ruling Grand Comnenos—a total of eleven, to be exact—were betrothed to Turkmen, to Mongol rulers and to emirs. It is only fair to say that the Grand Comneni did not invent the practice. They took their cue from Byzantium, where in 1346 Theodora Cantacuzene married the Ottoman ruler Orhan.

The arrangements surrounding these marriages were rather vague: the ceremonies took place outside the Empire and it is not clear whether a dowry or a bride price was ever paid. According to the Church the unions were invalid and Pope Pius II went as far as to say that the demise of the Empire of Trebizond was a clear sign of divine displeasure at such dealings. Ibn Battuta, on the other hand, saw the princesses as something akin to high commissioners in an allied court, protectors of local Christians. That may have been the case with Theodora Grand Comnena, who married the Ak Koyunlu chief Uzun Hasan and went on to live with her Greek entourage (which included a suitable complement of monks) in the fastness of Harput. She was his principal wife, his *hatun*, but unfortunately, when the crunch came, Uzun Hasan made no move to assist his father-in-law against the Ottomans. No other such bride ever attained the position of *hatun*; it shows that from a Turkish point of view, the princesses were hostages. None of them gave birth to the next ruler, thereby acquiring the powerful position akin to a *Valide Sultan* in the Ottoman court. Even so, they were clearly sought after. Their story does not appear in the Greek Pontic ballads but is recalled in the sixth ballad of *Dede Korkut*, a Turkmen folk cycle. It is set in 14th-century Trabzon in the Meydan and tells the story of the brave Han Turalı, one of the Ak Koyunlu Turkmen, and his quest for Salcan, a true Amazon of a princess who could draw two bows at a time and had already disposed of 32 previous suitors. It all ends happily but the Herculean labours the young Han Turalı has to perform go a long way to show how desirable she was.

The only Pontic girl who truly 'married well' was not a princess at all. Known as Maria de Doubera, she was the daughter of a converted Pontic Greek (or so one can infer from her name); her family was from the Matzouka Valley and had been able to assemble small estates, make its way in society and participate in local government. She married the Ottoman Sultan Beyazıt II in 1463 and was his principal wife. Her son Selim became Sultan Selim I (Yavuz Selim, the 'Grim'), but she was never *Valide Sultan* as she died before his accession. She took the name of Gülbahar; her mosque and *türbe* are in Trabzon.

In Europe a Trapezuntine princess graces the walls of the Pellegrini chapel in Sant'Anastasia, Verona. It is a work by Pisanello dated to the mid-15th century and represents either the liberation of the princess by St George or his departure to get his dragon. Either way, she looks magnificent in her finery and outsize headdress. In the background Trabzon looms high: all its fabled towers are there, with the inevitable gallows for the Turks to hang from. Cervantes must have had that picture in mind when he modelled his Dulcinea on a captive princess in need of a saviour; he would have had plenty of time during his five-year captivity in a Turkish prison in Algiers to hear about the folklore of his jailers.

As time progressed, Trapezuntine princesses became progressively ethereal and unreal. In Offenbach's comic opera *La princesse de Trébizonde,* she is not even a real person. Her wax image is sufficient to steer the deepest feelings in the male lead. But the opera was a great success, notwithstanding such arias as 'I have a toothache'; it was premiered in Paris in 1869 and went on the take Melbourne by storm in 1874.

Economically the Empire had a solid agricultural basis which accounted for three quarters of its wealth. Comparatively densely populated, it produced wine, wheat, olive oil, fruit, nuts, honey and wax well beyond subsistence level and exports boomed. Good timber was plentiful. Trabzon's main market was the Black Sea area. Trade to the east revived with the *Pax Mongolica*, when the Empire was a tributary of the Il Khans up to the mid-14th century; the Mongols encouraged land trade and when they sacked Baghdad in 1258, caravans took a different route via Tabriz, Erzurum and Trabzon. Tabriz was then their summer capital and the main city of the Il Khanate. The operation may have been in the hands of the Genoese and of the Venetians, but the Grand Comneni drove a hard bargain, taking a six percent profit on trade revenues, while in Byzantium the same Genoese and Venetians paid nothing at all to the local ruler. All this, added to mineral resources such as alum from Şebinkarahisar and iron from the Chalibian black sands, produced enough revenue for a rebuilding of the city to fit its new, elevated status.

Status was important to the ruling Grand Comnenos too, who aspired to be recognised as the only Byzantine emperor (at that time there were three rulers who styled themselves thus: one in Bithynia, another in Epirus and a third in Trabzon) and entertained the notion that he would be crowned in Byzantium in Haghia Sophia. When it became clear after 1261 (with the retaking of Constantinople from the Latins) that this was not going to happen, suitable arrangements had to be made. The Grand Comnenos formally renounced the title of 'Emperor of the Romans' and settled for 'Emperor of All the East'. The church of the Panaghia Chrysocephalos in the middle citadel was restored and partly rebuilt to fit the occasion.

The Comneni were keen to recreate a 'little Byzantium' in every sense. They were sticklers for etiquette, court ceremony and titles. They also took after the Byzantines in their passion for intrigue, deceit and murder. The inhabitants of the town responded in kind, by developing a reputation as practitioners of magic and the dark arts. The end of this Shangri-la Empire (to quote a leading Byzantinist) was swift. No cannons were fired and the casualties were few. After Byzantium had fallen to the Ottomans, the Trapezuntines scanned the sea (the sea being the road from Istanbul). And in fact Mehmet II did send a fleet, but that was only part of his plan. Just as he had surprised the Byzantines by getting his ships into the Golden Horn, circumventing the chain that closed it, so he took the Trapezuntines unawares when he appeared with a full army from the south. The Ottoman army had left Edirne five months before and now was the time. Emperor David surrendered on August 15th 1461. The promised help from his Ak Koyunlu son-in-law Uzun Hasan did not materialise. Trabzon became an Ottoman city.

TRABZON UNDER THE OTTOMANS

The Turks gradually occupied the walled area and non-Muslims remained outside. Trade dwindled. The Black Sea became a closed Ottoman lake. Only the Genoese and the Venetians retained some waning commercial interests. Trabzon was peripheral again, though it revived with the silver trade from Gümüşhane (*see p. 33*). It concentrated on supplying Istanbul with coffee, linen, butter, honey, fruit, nuts and rice as well silver, on fending off attacks from the east and on shipbuilding. Times became hard for non-Muslims, but the Matzouka Valley, where the monasteries retained their privileges, was a refuge and many moved to its relative safety, climbing ever higher into the valley to the limit of the Pontic range, above the tree line.

The sea opened up again under international pressure in the 19th century and for a short while Trabzon experienced a period of great prosperity, largely helped by the building of a carriage road to Tabriz. Eastern goods were back in fashion. The Crimean War had another positive effect on trade, and Trabzon began to compete with Tbilisi. The organisation of the trade was not in Greek hands but they provided the finance and it boomed. Trabzon was once again a cosmopolitan city. It acquired a theatre house, a casino, a local newspaper, an opera house, a night club and a number of fine mansions built by Greek bankers: the **Trabzon Museum** (in the centre; *open Tues–Sun 9.15–5.45; charge*) and the **Atatürk Köşkü** (*up in the hills to the south; signposted; open daily 9–7; 9–5 in winter; charge*) are two of them, both more interesting as mementoes of a recent past than for their contents. The days of the boomtown were not long. The opening of the Suez Canal was one nail in its coffin, followed by the construction of a port at Basra on the Persian Gulf. Trade suffered. The foreign consuls became redundant. The end came swiftly with the population exchanges of the 1920s.

EXPLORING TRABZON: FATİH CAMİİ (PANAGHIA CHRYSOCEPHALOS)

Panaghia Chrysocephalos (*map Trabzon*) was originally a monastery church that owed its name ('Golden Head') to the gilded bronze tiles of its roof (now covered in lead). The original church, a barrel-vaulted basilica with a pentagonal apse, became the coronation and funerary church of the Grand Comneni. It acquired a

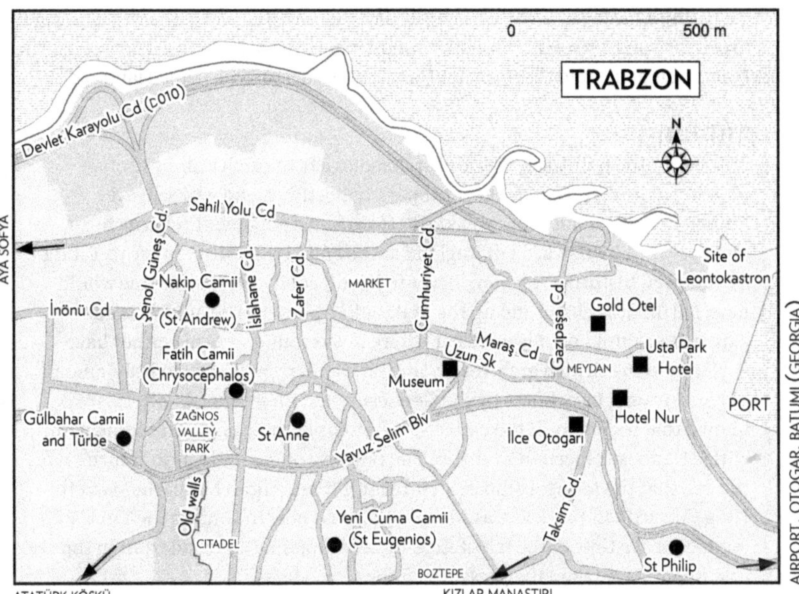

dome and a *metatorium*, or robing room, was added, as well as a large central pulpit where the coronation ceremony could be performed and a gallery for the new emperor to appear at and be acclaimed, accessed by a private staircase from the robing room. The church also possessed a luxurious copy of the Gospels (donated to Tsar Alexander II in 1858). In 1461 the building was turned into a mosque, the Fatih Camii, 'Victory Mosque', to commemorate Mehmet II's conquest of this corner of Christendom. The church's wall paintings were whitewashed over, its *opus sectile* floor was covered with wood (so it is not possible to see where the pulpit stood), the Comneni graves were destroyed and alterations were made to insert a *mihrab* and accommodate a new entrance with a wooden porch. The last surviving grave of a Grand Comnenos was that of Alexios IV, which stood outside the mosque until 1918. It was saved by its secondary use as the burial place of a local hero of the Muslim conquest, a shepherd named Hoşoğlan, who was apparently the first to enter the city on August 15th, 1461. After the monument was excavated by the Russians in 1916—and indeed they found one sarcophagus of reused marble slabs and two skeletons (one inserted later)—the remains of the emperor were handed over to the Greek community and eventually interred in the monastery of Nea Soumela in Veroia in northern Greece. The monument was later destroyed by the Turks.

The **imperial palace** was a two-storey building, north of the church in the upper citadel. Not much of it survives—which is a shame, since Lynch could still see important remains, including a wall with large pointed windows, when he visited at the beginning of the last century. The despot Andronikos, the illegitimate son of Alexios III, met his fate by being thrown out of one of those windows in 1376.

The **walls** of the lower town ran along today's Şenol Güneş Cd to the west and Zafer Cd to the east, and a sea wall closed the circuit where the Sahil Yolu Cd now runs. The harbour stretched out to the north and is now buried under reclaimed land.

THE EMBASSY

It is rarely given to historians and archaeologists to catch a glimpse of people's daily diet. Food is the most perishable thing, and who will ever bother to write about their breakfast? However, a document relating to an embassy sent by Edward I of England at the end of the 13th century to Tabriz has allowed historian Anthony Bryer to have a good look at what one would have fed on in Trabzon and up the Matzouka Valley and beyond. It is an expense account and it is not clear where it was found. It could either have surfaced in the British archives or, since it was first published in Italy, among papers brought back home by the Genoese when their officials left. It is known that members of the embassy left items of their luggage at some point with a Genoese official in Trabzon. The purpose of the trip was to return the call that the Mongol ambassador from Il Khan Argun had earlier sent to King Edward I in Bordeaux as well as to discuss how to contain the Turkish menace at the time of the fall of Acre in 1291. Opening a second front in the east might have taken the pressure off the Crusaders.

The embassy, some 20 people, passed twice through Trabzon in June/July 1292 and on the way back home in October of the same year. They visited the Il Khan in his summer capital, Tabriz. When they were on the coast their diet was quite varied, with olive oil, cereal, fish, nuts and fruit. The bulk of their expenditure, however, was meat (one quarter of the total) and wine (a prodigious 36 percent). They appear to have spent no money on vegetables. As they progressed inland, their diet became more spartan, most of their money going on bread with a bit of lard. On July 22nd 1292 they crossed the Pontic Gates and camped on Mount Karakabandağ (the *Kampana* of the Greeks), which they referred to as *Cabaneum*. Here they were above the tree line, in the highlands inhabited by transhumant shepherds. Bread could not be had: nomads do not have ovens and grow no cereals. They were able, however, to secure some milk and meat. On the way back they did some souvenir shopping in Trabzon, which included linen and an astonishing number of boots, 146 pairs, suggesting to Anthony Bryer that they were either very good or very bad quality. Some money went on buying a new lock for the cage of the leopard that was to be their companion all the way to Dover. The Il Khan must have thought it a suitable present for the King of England (who had leopards on his standard) in return for his falcons.

TRABZON'S CHURCHES AND MOSQUES

The Grand Comneni saw themselves as patrons of the Church and of the arts. Recent analysis of the written sources has come up with a total of 56 Comneni churches and over 20 monasteries in town (Orthodox, Armenian, Franciscan and Dominican).

Twenty-two Byzantine churches are known, of which only one remains standing today: the very plain church of **St Anne**, dating to the end of the 9th century as the worn inscription above the door states. The church, with a central nave and two aisles separated by two rows of reused Classical columns, was in use until 1923. It is normally not accessible.

Of the churches of the Empire period, a few have survived because they were turned into mosques; all incorporate some Classical architectural elements and were probably painted inside, but they are now whitewashed. Others fell victim to the zeal of the religious authorities when Trabzon went through a period of prosperity in the 19th century. Particularly notable is the **Yeni Cuma Camii** (formerly St Eugenios, a monastery church dedicated to the patron saint of the town martyred by Diocletian in 292). Here Mehmet II prayed soon after the conquest in 1461. It was originally a basilica and was rebuilt as a cross-in-square with the addition of a dome after being burnt down in a bout of civil strife in 1340. Indeed its location, close to the town and to invaders from the east, made it particularly vulnerable. The building is erratically signposted from Yavuz Selim Blv. Cross the road and take the steep climb south. It is a fine building with a couple of crosses set in the masonry. The inside, decorated with calligraphic inscriptions, has been whitewashed and is full of light. **St Philip** and the **Nakip Camii** (St Andrew) are also worth mentioning, though they perhaps do not merit a visit. Generally speaking, Trabzon's churches incorporated an eclectic mixture of styles: Byzantine (mosaics, *opus sectile* floors and painting) Georgian (large porches), Armenian (domes), Seljuk Anatolian (barrel vaulting), Russian and Balkan (mosaics and, according to travellers' reports, exterior painting).

Gülbahar Hatun Camii and türbe, the mosque and mausoleum of Maria de Doubera (*see p. 16*), mother of Sultan Selim I, are both off İnöü Cd, where the road starts climbing. The mosque is in the traditional Ottoman style with a large porch at the front. The mosque, but not the türbe, can be visited outside hours.

AYA SOFYA

Outside town a couple of kilometres to the west, in an area that was formerly fields and pastures but is now built up, is the Comneni's answer to Haghia Sophia in Byzantium, the Church of Divine Wisdom, a version built in stone rather than brick. The building (*beyond map Trabzon; it is possible to walk there, but any dolmuş heading west will also be fine; the driver will know*) was part of a monastery complex. Now only the church and its bell tower survive. It is no longer a church: for many years it was open as a museum but has recently been turned into a mosque, among much controversy—though that is certainly a better use for it than when it functioned as a military store in the 19th and 20th centuries and then as a hospital at the time of a cholera epidemic.

Visiting the building

Aya Sofya Camii, as the former church is now known, can be visited—indeed the whole area is being landscaped to create some welcoming greenery, and there are a couple of tea houses for refreshment. Note nearby a collection of mainly Roman remains (columns and other architectural remains), the result of rather hasty excavations along Uzun Sk, the main thoroughfare of Roman Trabzon. Unfortunately the advance of concrete has been relentless and Aya Sofya is cut off from the sea by the wide and busy coastal road. If you come here as a visitor rather than a worshipper, it is best to avoid Fridays. Note that inside, the nave has been carpeted and a false ceiling of cloth hides the frescoes, though you can catch a glimpse of them by standing in the apse. The narthex can still be admired. The bell tower is now fitted with loudspeakers and the dome is topped by a crescent moon. The description below mentions all the famous frescoes, including those no longer visible, or barely so.

History and description of the church

The church of Haghia Sophia at Trabzon, dating to the time of Manuel I (1238–63), was restored and extensively studied under the direction of David Talbot Rice in the 1960s. It stands on a podium with niches for tombs at the north and south ends. The foundations of an earlier smaller church are exposed to the north. The plan is a cross-in-square with a large dome. To the west the entrance is through a spacious narthex which spans the width of the building. It has a small chapel above. The central dome on a high drum is supported by four columns in Proconnesian marble. The fine *opus alexandrinum* floor under the dome is a combination of *opus sectile* and mosaic. At the east end, the central apse is flanked by two smaller apses. Two large porches incorporating architectural elements from an earlier building, possibly Hadrians's early 2nd-century temple to Apollo, have been built on the north and south sides. They show how close Georgia and Armenia are, not just in the idea of a porch in itself, but also in terms of the decoration; this is no standard Pontic church. The much worn **south porch frieze** is of particular interest, with the scene from Genesis running right to left (for emphasis?) while the writing (in Greek) runs in the opposite direction. It presents a misogynistic view of the Fall, with Eve taking all the blame. But there is salvation at hand, at least according to the Byzantinist Anthony Eastmond. He focused on the sequence leading through the south entrance with a Comneni eagle on the keystone, to the fresco of the Passion and Redemption in the nave and on to the pictorial decoration of the north porch centred on Mary, the mother of God (just as Eve in the other porch is the mother of Man). In his view this could be a structured processional route, an alternative to the main entrance to the west.

The **frescoes**, with their clarity and purity of colour, made Haghia Sophia justly famous. The main scenes are as follows. Over the door to the narthex are the *Agony in the Garden*, the *Last Supper* and the *Washing of the Feet*; over the main door, an angel with the veil of St Veronica; in the central vault, angels and the four Evangelists; on the vault of the south bay, the *Wedding Feast at Cana*, the *Healing of the Paralysed Man*, and *SS Sergius and Bacchus*; on the side wall the *Casting out of the Evil Spirit*, in the north bay *Christ Calming the Storm*, *Walking on the Water* and *Healing St Peter's Mother-in-Law*. On the central dome is Christ Pantocrator, with the Apostles and prophets in the drum. In the main apse are the *Annunciation* and the *Visitation*, and the *Ascension of Christ*. The grave of Manuel I is said to be under the south apse.

The much restored **bell tower** was started by Alexios IV in 1426 and possibly completed by his son John IV (1429–58), who was probably responsible for his death. It stands four storeys high. The ground-floor entrance led to a chapel with a painting of the Virgin extending her arms to the two above-mentioned emperors and thereby conferring legitimacy on both. The first floor also housed a chapel. But the entrance was outside: it was not part of the original plan. Its painted decoration, with scenes from the life of Christ, has been dated to c. 1442. It has been suggested that this second chapel had been willed by Emperor John as an act of expiation. The bell tower is now a minaret and cannot be visited.

THE REST OF THE TOWN

Our knowledge of the history of the rest of the town is patchy. At the time of the Empire, it developed on top of the previous settlement in the east, between the citadel and the sea. The east harbour (today the only harbour) was built up mainly for the use of Frankish (i.e. Western European) traders. The Genoese secured an excellent position for their headquarters and stores. They built their **Leontokastron**, possibly converted from an old convent, on the elevation overlooking the harbour. The area, which for a long time was in the hands of the military, is now a tea garden (though the military still occupy part of it). Some undated defensive architecture can be seen. It has not been investigated. The Venetians (*see below*) never had anything as grand. Their walled quarters with a defensive position, possibly a castle, were a smaller affair by the seaside.

The **Meydan** was used by the emperor for public appearances (*prokypsis*, a sort of *tableau vivant* of the imperial family) and also for camels and mules to assemble and prepare to take the caravan route to Tabriz (32 days), which started with the climb to Boztepe to the south along today's Taksim Cd. Several centuries later the Meydan is still the centre of town. There are cafés and eateries all around it and people use it like a village square, as a place to sit and chat. To the west of town, where the present-day stadium is, there was a polo pitch, a *tzykanisterion*. We know of its existence through written sources. Grand Comnenos John I Axouchos died there during a match in 1238.

South of the city on the slopes of **Boztepe**, the ancient Mount Mithrion, the monastery of the Panaghia Theoskepastos, locally known as **Kızlar Manastırı**, was founded c. 1340 by Empress Irene, incorporating an earlier cave sanctuary dedicated to the Persian god Mithras (similar to the church of San Clemente in Rome). It functioned until 1923; it has lost its roof and is now open to the elements but restoration work has recently been carried out. Only a shell is left, but the views out to sea across the rooftops are wonderful. The cave sanctuary is also still there. The nearby **Kamaklı Manastırı**, which had a community of Armenian monks until about the same date, has been turned into a farm. The small chapel has remains of interesting 17th-century frescoes.

THE LURE OF THE BLACK SEA: THE VENETIANS

For Venice the Black Sea was part of a wider involvement in maritime trade in the Mediterranean and beyond. Both Genoa and Venice were commercially active in Trabzon, but while the merchandise exchanged was roughly the same (weapons, silver and cloth were traded for slaves, furs and luxuries from the east), the organisation was quite different. In Genoa trade was very much in private hands and lightly regulated. Not so in Venice, where commerce was truly a state affair. Convoys of two to four galleys with a military escort (known as *mudae*) were organised yearly to reach the distant shores where Venice had either a colony or a trading interest. Destinations ranged from London, Bruges and Southampton (*muda di Fiandra*) to north Africa and Spain (*muda di Barbaria*) in the west, to Cyprus and Beirut (*muda di Siria*) and Byzantium and the Black Sea (*muda di Tana e Romania*) in the east. The Venetian senate allotted routes by auction to private consortia, whose freedom of action was constrained. Ships had to set sail at specific dates and follow prearranged routes. The senate also supervised the merchandise to be traded, the composition of the crew and the appointment of officers on board. There was, for instance, no winter sailing for Venetian ships, while the Genoese did occasionally take that risk. Venice had had a head start in the Black Sea trade after its pivotal role in the setting up of the Latin Empire (following their sack of Constantinople in 1204). The Black Sea was then too troubled for organised trade; indeed the warring Tartars had prevented Marco Polo's father and uncle from returning to Venice, so they pushed on east and ended up in China.

When the Byzantine rulers staged a comeback, ousting the Latins in 1261, they obviously favoured Genoa. For the next 200 years Genoa and Venice were to be in a constant state of friction over supremacy in the Black Sea and in the eastern Mediterranean, friction which erupted at least four times into open warfare. In the Black Sea, Venice had commercial outposts in the Crimea at Soldaia (now Sudak), in Trabzon (though nothing as grand as Genoa's Leontokastron) and in a few other coastal towns. It had a notary in Tabriz as early as 1264, as attested by legal documents. It all came to an end in the mid-1400s with the opening up of new sea routes and the transformation of the Black Sea into an Ottoman lake. Venice's commercial interests lingered on in the eastern Mediterranean until the beginning of the 18th century. As for Genoa, it had lost its independence by the mid-15th century.

PRACTICAL TIPS

GETTING THERE

By air: Trabzon Airport (close to town to the east; *www.trabzon.dhmi.gov.tr; T: 462 328 0940*) has connections to Istanbul (both airports) and Ankara. The best way to get into town from the airport is to walk to the main road and hail a *dolmuş*, or you can take a taxi.
By bus: Trabzon's *otogar*, with services to a wide variety of destinations, is on Devlet Karayolu to the east of town. It is best to take a *dolmuş* to/from the centre to avoid the wearying walk along the busy main road. The *otogar* also handles buses to Georgia. For local *dolmuş* services, enquire at the tourist office on Atatürk Alanı (the Meydan) or at the *ilce otogar*.

WHERE TO STAY

The main area for accommodation is around the Meydan (Atatürk Alanı), avoiding the less reputable hotels by the harbour. For an inexpensive option you can choose between **Hotel Nur** (*Cami Sk; T: 462 323 0445*) and **Otel Benli** (*Meydan Cami Sk; T 462 321 1750*). Both are next to the same mosque so you will be wakened by the call to prayer in the early hours of the morning. Alternatively, try **Gold Otel** (*İbrişoğlu Sk; T: 0462 321 2090*) north of the Meydan. They do not offer breakfast but there is an excellent pastry shop, Ustam, at the north end of the alleyway. The **Usta Park Otel** (*www.ustaparkhotel.com*) is a more comfortable and expensive alternative.

WHAT TO EAT

Eating places in Trabzon are mainly concentrated along Uzun Sk and on the Meydan. Keep an eye out for *kuymak* (probably of Georgian origin), a sort of fondue made with milk, cheese and cornflour and served with the local maize bread. It is very filling. One portion easily does for two people. Otherwise the thing to eat in Trabzon is *hamsi* (*see below*), prepared according to any of the 40+ recipes that exist, though what is most typically available is *hamsi tava*, in which the little fish are floured and cooked in a single layer in a frying pan.

HAMSİ

For the Turks, the *hamsi* is much more than a fish; it is a national treasure, a totem inspiring a multitude of feelings which have little to do with food. What other fish has humorous magazines named after it? At the last count, the *hamsi* had three. The little fish long ago captured the Turkish imagination. Evliya Çelebi can't resist making repeated allusions to the male member. 'What it 15cm long, slippery, purplish and lively?' he seems to ask. The *hamsi* of course—but we all know the real answer.

For the rest of us the *hamsi* is the anchovy (*Engraulis encrasicolus Cuv.*), which in the Black Sea was once found in astonishing quantities. Pliny the Elder (*31.44.95*), and the ancient Greeks before him, believed it to be bred from the rain, which explained its profusion. Its migration route has been known since antiquity; and whether or not it really did throw itself onto the beach (like a lemming in reverse), it has always been easy to catch at the right time with a light and a cage. It is strongly associated with Trabzon and must have contributed to the pickled fish and garum trade, for which the Black Sea was famous in antiquity. The arrival of the shoals was an event that warranted public notification, so that everyone could rush to the market. But quite what to do with such a bonanza? Gutted and salted, it will last up to two years, and as garum (which is fermented) probably forever. Over the centuries recipes have multiplied. There is the *hamsi pilaki*, an olive oil stew with layers of fish, onion, leek, parsley and cinnamon. Alternatively you can eat it sweet, as *hamsi baklava*. There are over 40 recipes to choose from.

But there is more to the *hamsi* than just a tasty meal. The little devil is of course an aphrodisiac. And *hamsi* heads can also be burnt for fumigation against vermin and to repel snakes. And if there are any left over, *hamsi* make excellent manure.

Today, partly because of these myriad potential uses, things are not looking so rosy for the *hamsi*. The ecology of the Black Sea is in deep trouble, not just because of pollution but also because of plain overfishing. The human population has increased enormously while the resources, be they land or fish, remain the same. The indiscriminate use of modern technology has temporarily boosted catches but seriously depleted stocks. And politicians prefer look at their ratings rather than tell their constituents not to fish. Things may have improved since Neal Ascherson's very negative assessment in his book on the Black Sea, but the road to recovery—if there is one—will be long.

FESTIVALS AND EVENTS

The famous **Kadırga Festivalı** offers singing, dancing, eating and many other forms of making merry. It takes place on the *yaylas*, the high pastures, and the location is different every year, as is the programme. If you happen to be around towards the end of July, enquire locally to get details.

The Matzouka Valley & the Trabzon Hinterland

The Matzouka Valley is situated directly south of Trabzon and its immediate hinterland, around the town of Maçka (*map C, 2*). Road signs today mark Gümüşhane and Erzurum: people now drive through the valley, not to it; it has ceased to be a destination in its own right. But this was not always so. In the past there was a strong synergy between Trabzon and its hinterland, with the valley people coming down to the city to sell their produce and the city inhabitants fleeing up the valley in times of danger.

The Matzouka differs from the other valleys that dissect the Pontic landscape in that it remained stubbornly Greek right up to the time of the population exchanges of the 1920s. While Greeks were a minority—though a powerful one—in Trabzon itself, there were c. 38,000 of them in the valley in the run-up to WWI, representing three quarters of the total population. Although the roaming nomadic Cepni Turkmen had settled in the Harşit Valley immediately to the west by the mid-14th century, they could never get a foothold here.

Topographically the Matzouka Valley is self-contained, protected to the south by the Pontic Alps, which at Deveboynu Tepesi reach over 3000m. There is talk of a Roman fort at Maçka, where the coin sequence is uninterrupted from the 1st century BC. One of the most densely populated areas of the Byzantine Empire, the valley has always been prime agricultural land, with enough rain and warmth to make anything grow. In antiquity cultivation was mixed, with olives, wheat, nuts, hemp and wine; later it was tobacco and maize. Summer pastures were at the south end. Here the Greeks came face to face with the nomadic Turks, who would look down on the lush greenness of the fertile valley's 'sea of trees' and compare it with a deep sigh to their own barren, bleak, windswept Anatolia. Settlement was mostly dispersed because of the steepness of the terrain, which could only be worked in terraces with a digging fork. Of the churches of the period, only Haghia Sophia at Leri, just over the crest (preserved because of its conversion into a mosque), is worth mentioning.

PONTIC GREEKS

It was as early as the 9th century of the present era that the Greek inhabitants of the Black Sea coast had to come to terms with their awkward position. Hemmed in between the mountains and the sea, attacked by the Arabs in the east and under pressure from the Persians, they soon realised that central power in Byzantium was distant and ineffective. The experience taught them the virtue of self-sufficiency, fostered a spirit of independence and of mutual solidarity, a tradition of self-government and clannishness, and a strong bond with the land from which they originated, even when they were physically remote from it. Moreover, while the authority of the Trabzon Empire came and went, that of the Orthodox Church (not the distant patriarch in Istanbul, but of the monasteries in the Matzouka Valley) remained strong to the last, because of historical circumstances.

There have been Greeks in the Pontus for over 2,000 years; one can say they have shaped much of its destiny as well as its landscape, with orchards and terraces on the steep valleys. The high points came partly at the time of the Trebizond Empire (*see p. 15*) but much more definitively in the period from the mid-19th century to c. 1910, under Ottoman rule. Those were the boom years for the coastal cities, with Samsun and Trabzon at the forefront. The Ottoman reform of 1856, granting equal status to all subjects, not only affected religion but also education and the economy as a whole. Greek speakers, who already had their own schools, reached out to the 'motherland', importing teachers from Athens, reconnecting with the Classical past and giving their children ancient Greek names. The financial boom was created by the reopening of the Trabzon-to-Tabriz route in 1830, the expansion of Samsun harbour, the exploitation of the Zonguldak coalfields and the tobacco business, which were all to a large extent in Greek hands. The Greeks had their own banks, newspapers and welfare associations, a Greek printing press and a number of consuls to appeal to and mobilise international public opinion. It is not surprising that this state of affairs did not win them many friends among the population at large, and their loyalty was repeatedly questioned. There are various cases in the 19th century of Greeks leaving before they were pushed. The Tsar sent welcoming signals from Russia, while frequently coming to blows with the Ottomans. The Greeks would leave in the wake of the retreating armies that they had welcomed as liberators.

Population statistics are unclear (there are no Ottoman censuses between 1590 and the 1880s and the relevant documentation from the monasteries has not been examined), but by the early 20th century the majority of the population was Muslim, with the Greeks making up around 20 percent. While the Greek population had remained static, the Muslims had quadrupled in number in 300 years.

With the dissolution of the Ottoman Empire the Pontic Greeks saw their chance—as did the Italians, the French and the British—to assume a portion of the spoils. The proposed Republic of Pontus, which was to stretch from Sinop to Batumi, was a direct result of President Wilson's 14 points. Number 12 called for the autonomous development of minorities in Turkey. The idea was discussed and then abandoned at the Paris conference of 1919.

The population exchanges of 1922–4 did little to solve an intractable problem. As the defining trait of a Turk is his religion, the exchange was organised along strict religious lines. For the Pontus, the net result of the departure of the Greeks was a skill shortage, a gap that took a long time to fill. Conversely, the new up-and-coming Turkish elite could easily lay their hands on fine abandoned properties and estates. According to some, the resulting social mix irrevocably set the tone of the newly-founded Republic as an authoritarian, one-party state. The economic and political elite (be it Greek or Armenian) was no longer there to provide a viable opposition.

In Greece the refugees were far from finding the motherland of their dreams; it simply did not exist. Their language, their manners and their customs were old-fashioned and set them apart from a resentful population who did not see them as Greek at all. There was no fraternisation, no welcome for the *tourkosporoi* ('Turkish seed') and the *yiaourtovaptismenoi* ('baptised in yoghurt'), especially in the towns. There were no lodgings, no jobs for them either. The Greek political landscape was to be deeply affected for a long time by this resentful, impoverished group stuck at the bottom of the pile. Things were marginally better in the countryside, especially in northern Greece, the part of the country from which the Muslim population had departed, at times leaving property and land behind them.

Today the Pontic diaspora has spread far and wide and strives to maintain its traditions, culture and language. It has its own *xenitia* songs lamenting the estrangement from the motherland: not Greece, the mother that did not want to recognise them as her own, but the southern shore of the Black Sea.

The Matzouka Valley began to develop at the time of the Empire of Trebizond, when the Grand Comneni extended their patronage to the religious establishments located there. Though there were only three of these in the valley, they prospered (albeit with serious ups and downs), faring better than the 15 or so religious institutions that Trabzon boasted. Most of the latter vanished with the Ottoman conquest, some so completely that only the names are left, as in the case of the Pharos Monastery. The Matzouka monasteries, on the other hand, **Vazelon**, **Sumela** and **St George Peristerota**, had a much longer life, continuing well into the 20th century. Historically this is a development that is difficult to explain since it appears to originate from an act of unexpected clemency form the newly-established Ottoman authority after the conquest in 1456. Although the monasteries lost some land, they were allowed to continue to exist and they developed into a truly economic as well as religious power. According to some, it was all the work of Maria de Doubera (*see p. 16*), who was born in the area and was the mother of Sultan Selim I. This is unlikely, because at the time when decisions about the future of Church holdings were taken, c.1465, she was still a child. The reason must lie somewhere else. The long tradition of the Pontic provinces of looking after their own affairs and not relying on the distant capital may have inspired the Ottoman authorities to allow the monasteries to continue to organise the local manpower into militias, into groups of agricultural producers and miners. As a result, while the coast became Turkish in this area, the hinterland remained predominantly Christian.

All three monasteries are perched on tall cliff faces, perhaps because of security considerations, or possibly simply owing to a desire for isolation; alternatively, more practical considerations may have prevailed in view of the dearth of cultivable land. Sumela is the most famous of the three monasteries today, though much reconstructed. Of the other two, there is little left to see. Vandalism, abandonment and neglect are to blame—but none of the above can destroy the stunning location and the views.

SUMELA MONASTERY

The Monastery of Sumela (*map C, 2*), or to give it its full name, the 'Holy Imperial Patriarchal and Stavropegic Monastery of the All Holy Mother of God on Mount Mela', is vertiginously situated halfway up a 300m sheer cliff overlooking the west bank of the Altındere river (the Panaghia) c. 48km south of Trabzon. It is located in what is now the Altındere Vadisi Milli Parkı (*open daylight hours, charge*). Access is via a steep, narrow path and a stairway. Much has been rebuilt and there is little left of the original splendour, but it is still a holy place, attracting both Christian and Muslim visitors, especially on the feast of the Dormition of the Virgin on 15th August.

Sumela's history began with a sacred cave and a holy icon. SS Barnabas and Sophronius came here from Athens with an icon of the Black Madonna (*Panaghia Atheniotissa*), said to have been painted by St Luke, and chose the cave as a congenial place to house it. The date of this first founding is hazy, somewhere between the 5th and the 10th century. We are on firmer ground with Alexios III Grand Comnenos (1349–90), because he left a *bulla* on the occasion of the refounding of the monastery in 1364; the document is now in Haghia Sophia in Istanbul. He also donated an icon of the Virgin Hodegetria, which in 1858 found its way to the National Gallery in Dublin. Both Alexios and his son Manuel III were crowned here and the monastery rose to become a substantial landowner, an economic power as the owner of whole villages, and a prodigious exporter of wine and oil. Over time it benefited enormously from the Gümüşhane silver mines, to which it supplied manpower for the mining works themselves and for the production of charcoal. This was not always an easy coexistence, as the enrichment of the monastery went hand in hand with the impoverishment of the peasantry, the *douloparoikoi*. The monastery had its ups and downs (there was a revolt by the put-upon labourers) and suffered from fires because of the wooden buildings. It continued to receive endowments in the Ottoman period, such as the grant from the Ypsilanti family who governed Wallachia for the sultan and originated in the valley. But by the beginning of the 19th century monastic discipline had broken down, there was a fall in numbers and monks were reduced to begging. Sumela successfully reinvented itself as an alternative *Hac* destination for Muslims who could not pay their way to Mecca, and continued in existence until 1916, when it was abandoned in the face of the advancing Russians. It never really recovered and was definitively vacated at the time of the population exchanges.

The buildings then became a target for treasure hunters (a number of precious items had been walled up in St Barbara Cave Church and were recovered in 1930) and for a time was used as a den for tobacco smugglers; there was another fire in 1930. The many treasures the monastery had accumulated over the centuries have now been dispersed; most of them are either in the Byzantine Museum in Athens or at Nea Sumela Monastery in Veroia in Greek Macedonia; some 150 manuscripts are in Istanbul but much material of that kind could not be saved and was left behind.

The present appearance of the monastery dates from the late 19th century, when the wooden monks' cells were replaced by a stone construction three to four storeys high; the frescoes outside the Great Cave Church, dating from the 18th century, were paid for out of the new wealth provided by the Gümüşhane mines. They are probably overlaid on top of earlier works. Inside are some earlier paintings, with a possible early 15th-century date (*being restored at the time of writing*). They depict some of the Grand Comneni from Andronikos III to Manuel III.

VAZELON MONASTERY

The monastery of Vazelon, dedicated to St John the Baptist, sits in an impregnable position on the slopes of Mount Zabulon overlooking a dense forest. (*NB: It is signposted to the west from the main road, in the middle of roadworks at the time of writing. After that there are no more signs and after the few villages on the slope have been passed, the road becomes very bad. It is advisable to travel with a guide.*) It is said to have been founded in 270 near a sacred spring, but the visible remains that you see today are 20th century reconstructions. Vazelon was also a Stavropegic monastery with substantial land holdings; its land was less productive than Sumela's, however, and the monastery was always poorer. It received endowments from the Grand Comneni Alexios III and Manuel III at the time of its refoundation, as attested in their *bullae* of the late 14th century, and subsequently by Peter the Great of Russia. In 1895 it was made over to Sumela and reorganised. Only the chapel dedicated to St Elias (the prophet Elijah) has survived from the original nucleus. Situated on a terrace 30m north of the main monastery building, it is a small barrel-vaulted construction with a single layer of frescoes that have been dated to the Grand Comneni Empire period.

ST GEORGE PERISTEROTA MONASTERY

This monastery, originally dating to the 8th century and known locally as Kuştul Manastırı, is also a Grand Comneni refoundation (1393). It sits on a rocky ledge in the wilderness. It can be reached by taking the side road east from Esiroğlu, 20km south of Trabzon on Route 885. The cave church of Peristera to the southwest of the monastery is said to have inspired its name. The alternative version refers to a legend in which a flock of doves (Greek '*peristeri*') showed the way to the spot to a group of monks carrying the icon of St George. Whatever the truth, Peristerota monastery went through many trials and tribulations and periods of abandonment; its buildings were destroyed many times and finally went up in flames in 1904. It was rebuilt, but only to be deserted in 1923. Throughout it retained its land holdings and Stavropegic status. Nothing remains of its 7,000-volume library, which perished in the fire. The roofless rooms of the monastery that remain today all post-date the fire. The church is no more.

THE LURE OF THE BLACK SEA: THE TEN THOUSAND

When Xenophon and his Ten Thousand caught sight of the Black Sea in 400 BC (to the famous exultant cry of '*Thalatta! Thalatta!*') it was not the end of their tribulations. They were c. 50km south of Trabzon on the Makur Dağı, west of Deveboynu Tepesi, from which the sea can clearly be seen. In later times the Roman emperor Hadrian followed in their footsteps, during his frontier inspection of AD 131. Information on his visit and instructions for a suitable commemoration (an altar and a statue of himself pointing to the sea) are contained in a letter by Arrian, who was then governor of the province.

After much rejoicing, embracing and dancing, the celebratory erecting of a cairn and votive offerings of wicker shields and untanned skins, the Greeks sent back their Armenian guide, a local man whom they handsomely rewarded. They then plunged into the wooded slopes. They were still quite a distance from home, but of course they knew that this was the Pontos Euxinos where a number of Greek colonies thrived; so, in a way, they were among friends—a marked change of fortune considering the inhospitable country they had crossed on their way from Cunaxa, deep in Mesopotamia. It seems that they were right to bank on the time-honoured traditions of hospitality: as they reached the sea, the Trapezuntines sent them gifts of oxen, wheat and wine. But theirs was a problem of numbers. They were officially 10,000 men (a few had probably been lost along the way) but at one point in Xenophon's narrative, the *Anabasis*, we read also of women and boys. This begins to look very much like a typical army, made up of soldiers and a trail of camp followers. There is no such thing as a tradition of hospitality that can sustain numbers of this size for an indefinite time. And though the people of Trabzon offered them a market so that they could buy their food, it seems that it was not enough: pillaging was probably easier. And while they were waiting for the return of Cheirisophos, who had been instructed to come back with enough sea transport, the merry band decided to ravage the hinterland. It proved to be no mean feat, as the terrain was all ravines and high peaks, but it had the desired effect of producing 'gifts of hospitality' and some loot. And so it went on as the soldiers made their way west. Food and transport were obtained by a combination of blackmail and offers of mercenary services to various cities and tribes. Indeed, their progression along the south coast can be compared to the handing over of a hot potato. Xenophon and his men eventually reached almost the end of the road at Heracleia, helped on their way by the merchants of Sinop, who provided the soldiers with pay so that they could buy their food when they got there. But the people of Heracleia had other ideas: after deliberating 'they got together their goods and chattels from their farms and fields outside, and dismantled the market outside and transferred it within, after which the gates were closed, and arms appeared at the battlements of the walls' (*6.2*). One is left to wonder what prompted such an unfriendly reaction: were the Ten Thousand seen as fellow Greeks or as roaming hungry mercenaries? Probably the latter. They eventually must have reached a compromise, because vessels were supplied and they all got home one way or another.

THE CHALDIA REGION

Over the Pontic Gates (2010m), roughly but not quite where Xenophon and his Ten Thousand first saw the sea (*see above*), the land drops to the region of Chaldia, in which the Harşit river (the ancient *Filavonitis*) flows west and then north, emptying into the Black Sea at Tirebolu.

There is controversy over the name Chaldia. Some relate it to the Urartians and their god Haldi, but there is little evidence of any Urartian involvement here. The Pontic Greeks called the local inhabitants *Chaldaioi,* but there is no Classical or late antique evidence for the name, and Xenophon's *Chaldaioi* are almost certainly not the same. It has been suggested that the name may have Armenian origins.

After the lush Matzouka Valley with its 'sea of trees' (the *ağaç denizi* that so impressed the roaming Turkmen when they caught sight of it) and its greenness betraying the abundant rain, Chaldia is a much harsher environment, with an agricultural cycle that is closer to that of the Anatolian plateau to the south. Trees are scarce: eucalyptus and poplars a recent introduction. The land has been stripped bare of its tree cover—if it ever had one—by the mining operations (*see below*). Rivers run dry in hot summers, but the watercourses can be prone to flash floods. Physical constraints have bred a strong local identity and self-reliance. This is traditionally a land of local warlords in their castles, leading a detached existence from the goings on in Trabzon or indeed in the City (Byzantium or Istanbul), though Chaldia was technically an imperial possession. Records show that while the Dukes of Chaldia served the Byzantines as generals, others offered their services to the Seljuks and some were occasionally on both payrolls.

Chaldia fell to the Ottomans later than Trabzon. The castle of **Torul** (*map C, 2*), which held out successfully against Mehmet II in 1461, only surrendered in 1480. Trade came through this way; tolls were duly levied, and plundering was part of the game. But the extraordinary economic boom experienced by the region in the 16th–18th centuries was caused by the mineral potential in its granitic volcanic subsoil. This was an important development for the region, since under the Ottomans the Black Sea was no longer used by international trading vessels and the caravan routes had closed.

GÜMÜŞHANE

According to the Comneni archives, the Trebizond Empire was self-sufficient in metals. It certainly required a fair amount of silver to pay the tribute to the Mongol overlord and to run the mint, and there appears to have been a lively gold- and silversmithing industry in the city. The source of that silver has not been securely located.

The first mention of a Gümüşhane ('House of Silver') refers to the fortress of Canca, where silver was first mined at the end of 16th century. The works may have been started by local Armenians but the land belonged to the sultan and by the 17th century things were organised on an industrial scale. The general administration was in the hands of salaried Muslims, but they quickly faded into the background. The master miner (the *archimetallurgos*) was the most important person in the operation: he was either a Greek or an Armenian. And since the monasteries of the Matzouka Valley provided the bulk of the workforce (miners and charcoal burners), their influence and possibilities of gain were immense.

The mines were vital to the sultan and indeed at their peak in the early 18th century they produced over 1,000 pounds of silver and 120 of gold annually. The master miner, a position that was handed down from father to son, had the ear of the sultan and could extract important concessions, such as tax exemptions for entire villages. Money was also made by the clandestine smuggling of precious metals and selling the lead that was a by-product of the extraction process. Operations were chaotically run. Workers moved to follow the metal, and meanwhile the all-important charcoal burners were destroying the landscape. It takes four pounds of wood to make one pound of charcoal and 2,000 pounds of charcoal are needed for every pound of silver.

By the end of the 18th century both the landscape and the mines were starting to show signs of exhaustion. Miners moved to Ergani (*map C, 6; see Blue Guide Southeastern Turkey*) or to Şebinkarahisar (*map C, 4*). The two Russo-Turkish wars of 1828 and 1877 led to a further diaspora. Chaldia was empty of wood and of silver. There was no money. The new school at Argyroupolis (*see below*) was paid for by melting down the silver votive offerings from the church. Notwithstanding this, at the time of the population exchanges, the silver treasure belonging to the church—which included a solid silver bishop's mitre—was still impressive (it can be seen in the Benaki Museum in Athens). The mines were officially closed in 1929 and the area has since become a fruit-producing district.

WHAT TO SEE AT GÜMÜŞHANE

Getting around can be confusing because of an overlap of names. The present town of **Gümüşhane** (*map C, 2*) dates from the early 20th century. Silver mining first began on the rock on the west side of the valley to the north (*signposted from the valley bottom*). Here was a Byzantine castle (*Tzanica*) which the Ottomans after 1479 called Canca; this explains why some coins from the short-lived mint are marked with that name. At Canca you can see the remains of a couple of churches (*though the road was closed at the time of writing*). From the end of the 16th century, a new town was developed in the vicinity and is accessible. The Greeks baptised it **Argyroupolis** ('Silver Town') in 1846 but it was known to the Turks as Gümüşhane; when present-day Gümüşhane was built, the previous one became known as Eski (Old) Gümüşhane. Today it goes by the name of **Süleymaniye** and is a small village dotted with incongruous ruins, the only stone houses in all the valley. The local mudbrick and wood building style, with its rounded corners, is quite distinct. The plan by the mosque is very helpful. Here were the Church of St George Megalomartyr, the Cathedral, the Bishop's Palace, the school and a number of well-appointed houses belonging to local worthies. Now nature has taken over: the butterflies are back. If you can, make time to visit the local museum at the top end of town, the **Gümüşhane İkizevler Konağı** (*open Tues–Sun 8.30–12 & 1–5*). It has interesting ethnographic material and the house itself is worth a look.

LERİ (YETİRMEZ)

Twenty-seven kilometres upstream from Gümüşhane to the east, in an area that formed a border between the Greeks and the Armenians, is a very interesting church, presently a disused mosque. The town of Leri (now the village of Yetirmez, 4km northwest of Kabaköy; *take the turn north to Arzular where the Aşkale Çimento factory is. Yetirmez is 3km up a winding road to the left after Arzular*) was for a short while in the 9th century the seat of a bishopric, a dependent of Trebizond. There is no further mention of it after 1094. The basilica, dedicated to Haghia Sophia, is a diminutive but well-proportioned 14m by 11m construction partly built of multicoloured ashlar limestone blocks. It would seem to be Armenian because of the semicircular apse, the rectangular pastophoria, and the stone barrel-vaulted ceiling supported by four columns, but it lacks a dome. So while it is not in the tradition of the medieval Trapezuntine churches, it is not completely Armenian either, or perhaps a mixture of Armenian and Anatolian traditions. It has tentatively been dated to the 6th/7th century, with alterations when Leri became a bishopric.

SATALA (SADAK)

South of Gümüşhane on the Erzincan–Kelkit road, 3km east of the village of Mahomatlı, is the village of Sadak (ancient *Satala*), quite high up at 1800m (*map C, 4*). In the 1st century AD the Roman border ran from *Melitene* (Malatya; *map C, 6*) to Trabzon via Satala. This was the edge of the Empire, at a time when it was poised to launch an aggressive policy towards the east. Satala controlled the possible Persian invasion routes, access to Trabzon and the supply port, as well as the Euphrates and Lycus plains. Moreover, the area was well watered and supplies could be obtained from the fertile Erzincan plain. The decision to build a permanent legionary camp (*castra stativa*) was taken by Vespasian in AD 75. This was to be one of the four Roman legionary fortresses in Anatolia, the others were at Zeugma, Melitene and Samosata (modern Samsat). Their brief was to guard a 500km frontier from the heart of Anatolia to the Black Sea.

A legionary fortress (some 400m by 420m) meant a large concentration—in the thousands—of soldiers on regular pay, plus a probably equal number of hangers-on: slaves, women and other camp followers eager to provide whatever was needed and who would settle or squat outside the walls. The presence of soldiers offered protection in troubled times and the supply of ready cash made trade possible. The transition from military settlement to town was inevitable. One hears of a bishop of Satala attending the Council of Nicaea in the early 4th century. The Byzantines used Satala for the same military purposes as the Roman had, and Justinian rebuilt it after yet another Persian attack. After its conquest by Khrusan the Victorious in 610, however, Satala seems simply to have fallen off the map. It is not heard of again.

The ruins first came to the attention of the outside world in 1873, when bronze fragments of a large statue of Aphrodite (the head is now in the British Museum) were found. The British Vice Consul in Trabzon, Alfred Billotti, paid a visit and carried out some excavations. The numerous stray finds and inscriptions suggest that early Satala was very much an outpost of Latin culture and that it gradually became more Greek, especially in the town that developed outside the walls. Stone-robbing has been a perennial problem. The 4th–5th-century Satala aqueduct, which brought water from the north and of which seven arches stood in 1866, is now reduced to a single arch and three piers; its revetment was removed to Erzincan in the 19th century and was used in government buildings. Plans are afoot for an exhaustive investigation, which will include the little-known civilian settlement. The layout of the Justinianian fortress is known and it is reputed that its double walls were 'higher than mountains'. Even so, it was smaller than than its predecessor. At the moment there is not a lot to see, The site is under pasture and cultivation (cereal, hopefully with some limit to the depth of ploughing). There has been a proposed investigation by a German team. Nevertheless, the sign to 'Satala Ancient City' is there and cannot be missed: the historical significance of the place is undeniable.

BAYBURT & İSPİR

East of Gümüşhane, Route 050 takes you deep into ancient Armenia. After the battle of Manzikert in 1071, this area was lost to the Seljuks; both Bayburt and İspir were towns with a large Armenian Christian population, but from the 11th century ruled by Muslim emirs. Both towns were on the caravan route to Tabriz and their connection with Trabzon was strictly commercial.

BAYBURT

What greets the modern visitor to Bayburt (ancient Paipert; *map C, 4*) is comparatively recent: a middle-sized market town with a riverside (the water perhaps none too clean) and a main street with its Atatürk monument leading to the foot of the Kale. The eateries (*lokantas* used by local people; very few tourists come here) are along here. The town is on a slope and the Kale, now empty, dominates it from the top of the rock to the south of the plain.

The circuit of the old walls is very large: it used to contain the whole settlement. After the destruction wreaked by the Russians in 1829, the population moved out. The castle is in a unique defensive position, well protected by its steep slopes and the Çoruh River (the ancient *Akampis*) on its northwest side. The reconstruction of the 1km-long wall circuit, with towers, by the Saltukid ruler Muğit al-Din Tuğrul Shah in the early 13th century, was very thorough: very little is left of whatever the

Byzantines, Armenians or Georgians may have built earlier. There followed the usual additions and alterations up to Ottoman times, with towers and double walls in places. The gatehouse, which was blown up by the Russians, is a reconstruction of 1970.

The floruit of Bayburt was in the 13th–14th centuries, when the Trabzon-to-Tabriz route was propsering. Both the Mongols and the Seljuks had a mint here. The Grand Comneni Empire also took an interest. The very ruinous castle church is on the Trapezuntine model, with a central apse, polygonal on the outside, and two side apses. According to Ottoman census documents, Bayburt retained a large Christian population and still had a bishop at the beginning of the 20th century. The Kale belongs to the birds and to the rare visitor. It is always accessible, though it does look much better from a distance.

İSPIR

Following the Çoruh as it doubles back on itself on the way to Batumi, the road leads to İspir (ancient *Sper*; *map C, 2*), a town with interesting houses built in dressed stone with wooden courses and topped by pitched roofs. The valley is fertile, but the altitude (1500m) means that only barley grows here. The Arabs took İspir in the 9th century, after which it is unclear whether it came into Georgian or Armenian hands. When the Seljuks in the early 11th century conquered it, the Christian population was spared, though that tolerance was not extended to the Greek Orthodox, who were banished. At the time of the Empire of Trebizond (*see p. 15*), this was yet another Christian state on its border (Christians made up almost 100 percent of the population), though the Christianity was Armenian rather than Greek. This was to become a familiar pattern in the Empire, and Greek Orthodox bishops moved to the coast from their inland sees.

The town of İspir is well separated from its Kale, which sits on a steep rock south of the river. Its defences belong to various periods up to the Ottoman era, and there has also been recent rebuilding. Inside the circuit, the church—already in a sorry state by the 1950s and now reduced to the apse, narthex and north wall, follows the Trapezuntine model. Built on a basilica plan, it had a central apse, pentagonal on the outside, and two smaller apses on either side of it. Despite this, it is difficult to imagine any influence from Trabzon here. Indeed, the two states (the Empire of Trebizond and the local emirate) were at war in 1223 and Trabzon was saved by a well-timed downpour brought about by its patron, St Eugenios. İspir is more likely to have looked towards Georgia, whose queen had married the son of its ruler. It has been suggested that the castle church and castle mosque were built roughly at the same time, in the 12th/13th century (the stone comes from the same quarry), probably by a Trapezuntine architect.

UZUNGÖL LAKE

Deep into the mountains, the village of Uzungöl, by the lake of the same name (which means 'Long Lake'; *map C, 2*), has become a famous beauty spot—though for much of the year it is swathed in mist and fog. In spring and summer it is extremely popular for its dramatic scenery, and also because the access roads are good and accommodation plentiful. If you are a keen walker, it is a good idea to find accommodation here, enjoy it in the evening and make day trips during the day, leaving behind the souvenir shops, the coaches and the concrete, which has been poured here in abundance.

PRACTICAL TIPS

GETTING THERE

Organised tours leave from Trabzon for Sumela Monastery: enquire at your hotel. You will need good footwear. The other monasteries require stout (4WD) private transport and possibly a guide. Both are signposted from the main road, but the side roads are terrible and the tracks and paths confusing.

Gümüşhane and Bayburt are both on the main route from Trabzon to Erzurum, and there are plentiful bus services to and from each. İspir is more remote. It can be reached on a *dolmuş* that traverses the Çoruh Valley, either from Artvin or from Erzurum.

WHERE TO STAY

We are here on the borders of the Kaçkar National Park, which is opening up to tourism. Places like **Uzungöl**, deep into the mountains, have possibly more accommodation than they need. Around the lake every single building seems to offer accommodation of a sort.

Both İspir and Bayburt offer reasonable choices. In **Bayburt** there is the Otel Bayburt (*T: 458 222 6969, www.otelbayburt.com*), very modern and somewhat out of the city centre. Right in the centre, almost at the foot of the castle, is the Çiçek Otel. It is very, very basic and very inexpensive but the hot shower is first class. Another basic choice in the centre is the Saraçoğlu Otel (*Cumhuriyet Cd 21; T: 458 211 7217*). In **İspir** the Kaçkar Otel (*25 Şubat Cd, Belediye Binası; T: 442 451 2949*), situated to the west of the castle, makes a good choice.

Gümüşhane has a number of hotels, but it is wise to endeavour not to get stuck here for the night. The town feels slightly chaotic and the addition of a brand new university (2008) has added to its traffic problems. Aim to get here early enough to visit the ruins and the museum, and then push on.

WHERE TO EAT

There is no difficulty getting fed in popular spots like Soumela and Uzungöl, but the food will be the kind of thing tourists are reputed to want to eat. In general the Turks like to eat out, to get out of the house and meet friends, and also to generate reciprocal business so that in due course, for example, the owner of the restaurant will come to their shop. For an authentic Turkish experience, the place to ask for is a *'lokanta'*. This will have a short menu, not posted up outside. You will have to take the plunge and hope for the best. You can see the food on offer and point at what you want. The atmosphere is friendly—extremely so for a foreigner as there are not many of them in these parts. The bill will be astonishingly small. Insist on sealed water (*kapalı su*) and avoid uncooked vegetables to be absolutely on the safe side.

LOCAL SPECIALITIES

When Gümüşhane abandoned mining, it reinvented itself as a fruit-producing area and has acquired a reputation for its fruit preserves. Its production of ***pestil*** and ***köme*** is protected by a Geographical Registration issued by the Turkish Patent Institute, which means that you have a good chance of finding the genuine article here. *Köme* is a sausage-shaped snack full of nuts and encased in a sticky, translucent film. *Pestil* is roughly the same thing, but it is flat. The glutinous mixture of starch, sugar, flour, honey, milk and a variety of fruits (mainly mulberry as well as grape, apple, and rosehip) is boiled and rendered down before being processed (a lengthy procedure).

Erzurum

South of the Georgian district *(described in Chapter 1)*, Erzurum *(map D, 3)* sits on a high lava plateau (1828m) on the edge of Asia Minor on a minor branch of the Northern Anatolian Fault *(see below)*. Recent fieldwork in the region to the northeast around Baldızı has identified the remains of a mega landslide complex with a median thickness of 150m and a surface c. 11km by 5km, which occurred, geologically speaking, in recent times. The area is far from quiet but this has not prevented Erzurum from prospering.

THE NORTHERN ANATOLIAN FAULT

Turkey is a land of earthquakes, nowhere more so than along the Northern Anatolian Fault, which runs from an obscure spot seemingly in the middle of nowhere directly south of Erzurum, on the way to Bingöl. Here, at the geologically famous **Karlıova Triple Junction**, the Anatolian, Arabian and Eurasian plates meet. As the Eurasian plate holds firm and the Arabian plate pushes north, the Anatolian plate is forever trying to escape west. Earthquakes have been frequent and devastating. The fault can be traced all the way to mainland Greece over 1000km away, following a contour line about 100km inland from the Black Sea coast. The depression has been colonised by a number of rivers, including the northern branch of the Euphrates (the Kara Su), which runs along it until it turns south after Erzincan. Both the Kelkit and the Yeşilırmak occupy it before heading north to the Black Sea. More tellingly, Route 100 also runs along it, showing it has always been an important means of east–west communication.

The northern branch of the Euphrates, the Kara Su, flows south of Erzurum. The Georgian Gates (Gürcü Boğazı), the scene of many bloody battles over the centuries, are just 35km away to the north on Route 950. The city however, was never in Georgian hands, although trade did flow in that direction, while over the centuries caravans went to and fro from Sivas and Trabzon to Iran. As a frontier city, trade has always been the calling of Erzurum (when not at war). Caravans assembled here either to continue due east along the northern route via Doğubayazıt, or south through Hinis and Lake Van. Fortunes depended on many things, first and foremost on the international situation, a fact which is reflected in the makeup of the city. In its heyday Erzurum was the chief city of East Asia and its pasha ranked second only to Baghdad's. Lynch, at the end of the 19th century, estimated that some 30–40,000 camels passed through the city every year.

HISTORY OF ERZURUM

Erzurum prides itself on being the highest city in Turkey—though in winter, this may seem little cause for rejoicing. It was planned as a military outpost by the Byzantines and the centre of town still retains the shape of the original soldiers' camp. It was called Theodosiopolis, after the Byzantine Emperor Theodosius II (first half of the 5th century). The citadel was where it is now, on the highest point; the walls were double, complemented by a ditch and pierced by four gates. James Morier, the author of *A Journey from Persia, Armenia and Asia Minor to Constantinople,* who was here in June 1809, commented on the bastions and the openings for cannons. He saw the city gates covered in iron sheeting and tanners and blacksmiths at work outside the walls by the ditch. Nothing now remains of the walls, nor of the gates, but their locations can be made out on a street plan. The city's Georgian Gate stood to the north, roughly where Gürcükapı Cd is, the Erzincan and the Tabriz gates were respectively at the west and east ends of Cumuriyet Cd and the Harput Gate stood halfway along Yenikapı Cd. The ring road around the old city follows the line of the walls. There does not seem to have been a previous settlement, although the region is fertile with good grazing land and commercial movement along the Kara Su Valley must have gone on since time immemorial. The area was certainly not empty: it was in the hands of the Armenians. When the Byzantines took control, Theodosiopolis was set up as the headquarters of the Count of Armenia, a Byzantine official charged with keeping an eye on the various Armenian lords, the *nakhrars*. Then, as the Byzantines finally lost control to the Arabs, the Armenians returned to the city from the nearby town of Artsan: a corruption of the designation 'Artsan of the Rum' (of the eastern Romans, i.e. the Byzantines) may be the origin of the present name of Erzurum (although there are other theories).

After the Arabs came the Seljuks and the Mongols. These were times of prosperity: trade boomed and striking monuments were erected. The Seljuks founded the Çifte Minareli Medresesi in 1230. With the arrival of the Mongols in 1242, Erzurum regained its military role as the summer headquarters of the Il Khan troops in Asia Minor (given the harsh winters, the troops must have been happy to decamp at the first hint of autumn). It was the Mongols who founded the wonderful Yakutiye Medresesi. After a spell under the Kara Koyunlu, Erzurum finally came under Ottoman rule in 1514 and its military character intensified. Janissaries occupied the citadel; only Muslim notables were allowed to reside within the walled area. Mosques and medreses replaced churches. The Armenians moved out to the suburbs and the city grew. The commercial headquarters relocated to the northeast, where the caravanserais and the customs building were, hence today's Gümrük (Custom) Cami there. Here James Morier had his luggage inspected.

In the 19th century, as a military outpost, Erzurum acquired additional fortifications, with a ring of forts one and a half miles to the southeast of the walled city. The old city walls were plundered for their well-cut stone. Other fortifications were built as far away as the Georgian Gates, in the Palandöken Mountains and on the Pasinler Plain. The railway came in 1939 and on the advice of a British architect, a certain Mr Lambert, the wide boulevard from the station to the Georgian Gate was carved through the suburbs. Today Erzurum retains a military presence, though the janissaries are long gone.

A WALK THROUGH TOWN

A visit to Erzurum is ideally begun from the top of the **clock tower** in the Kale. It is easily found: the citadel is the only elevation in an otherwise flat landscape. From the top of the tower you can get your bearings and enjoy a wide panorama, with the plateau gently melting into the hills in the distance. (*NB: At the time of going to press, the clock tower was not accessible; it is up to you to decide whether you want to pay the entrance fee for the citadel; there is not great deal to see—the view from the clock tower is by far the main attraction—but a short description is given here*). Excavations within the citadel show little beyond the foundations of Ottoman barracks. The tower and the mosque were originally built by the Saltukids (the local Seljuk rulers); the tower was intended as a minaret, but by the 17th century it housed a cannon that boomed at appropriate times to guide the faithful in their Ramadan devotions. In the 18th century came the clock, which chimed on the hour, and later a wooden cover and a *şerefe* were added. After the clock broke down, the Russians removed it in 1830. A new clock (manufactured in Croydon) was offered by the British Government. It was installed in 1881; in the process the Saltukid inscription referring to the building of the tower was damaged.

The **Çifte Minareli Medresesi**, in the southeast corner of the old town, was built by Hundi Hatun, daughter of Alaettin Keykubad, the local Seljuk ruler, around the middle of the 13th century; it was never finished. Its portal is framed by two minarets, hence its name (*çifte* means double, or a pair). This was a great time for this style of building: it is thought that this medrese was the model for the stunning Gök Medrese in Sivas, built in 1271. Its life has been hard, however. By the 16th century it was no longer a medrese but was used as a gun foundry. Its past role as a medrese had been forgotten and it was believed instead to have been a mosque. Later it endured a spell as an arsenal and a store for cannon balls. This was followed by a period of disuse in the early 20th century. Its plan is rectangular, with an extension to the south for a large and empty mausoleum, thought to have been built for Hundi Hatun. The courtyard is taken up by a two-storey portico with two *iwans* on the long sides. At the south end, the *iwan* is larger and deeper; the style of the architecture is different here, as is the building stone. It has been suggested that it may be part of a previous monument or perhaps even a false start. The abundant carved decoration remains unfinished. At the front the minarets have blue tiles with fluted brickwork. The calligraphic medallion set in a square contains the names of Allah, Mohammed and the four Companions of the Prophet. On the outside, the east wall of the medrese abutted the city wall, and indeed a pentagonal tower belonging to the latter was incorporated in the structure of the *iwan*. Whether it will survive the relentless programme of road-building and widening remains to be seen. The monument was closed for restoration at the time of writing.

The **Yakutiye Medresesi** was commissioned by the local Mongol governor Khwadja Yakut for the Il Khan Oljaytu in 1310. It is situated next to the Lala Paşa

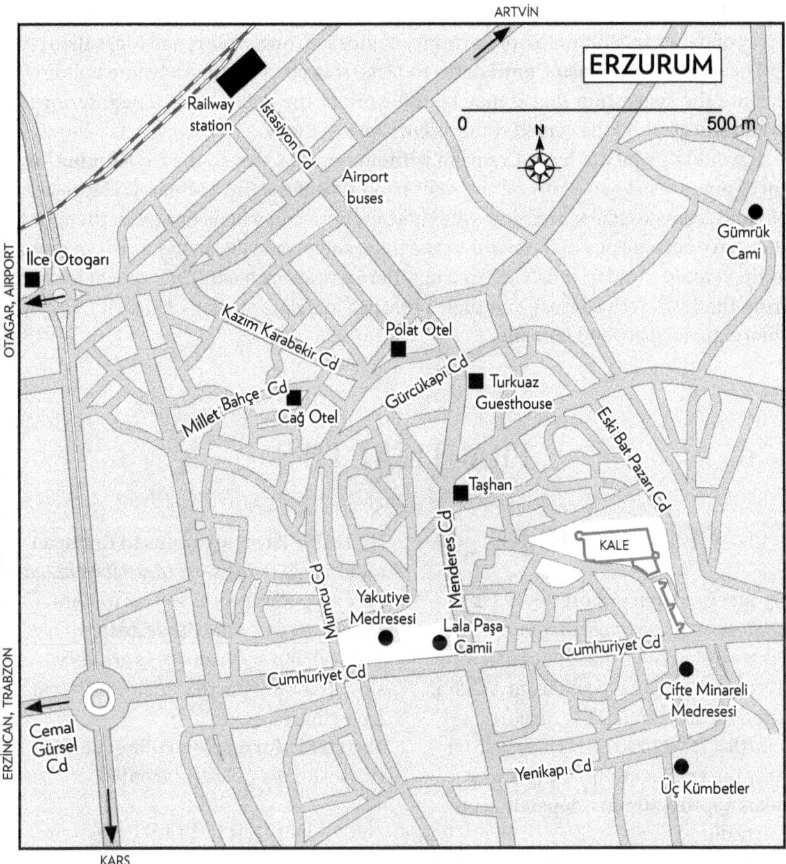

Mosque. It was originally a double minaret medrese but only the south minaret is still standing. A long period of neglect is to blame: the building was used as a gun foundry when works were moved here from the Çifte Minareli Medresesi in 1837, but as the entrance proved too small for carts, the upper chamber of the *türbe* in the northeast corner was cut. Later the area was used by the army and the medrese was surrounded by barracks. The surviving minaret (entered from the roof), with its zig-zag decoration in turquoise and darker tiles (a colour achieved with the addition of manganese), is striking despite the loss of its original crown. The exuberant portal is decorated by two trees of life framing a double-headed eagle. Uncharacteristically for a medrese, the inner space is completely covered with three *iwans* set between engaged pillars. The *türbe* (which appears unused) at the end is bonded to the wall of the medrese; the two are therefore contemporary. The monument has been restored and is now a museum (*open daily 9–5; charge*) exhibiting local ethnic items such as a set of 12th-century Rufai needles, which were used by the faithful to inflict pain upon themselves at public events. The souvenir shop at the top end offers the usual array of goods and affords an opportunity to stock up on Snickers and Mars Bars.

The nearby **Lala Paşa Camii** dates to 1563. It is not a particularly fine building, despite the suggestion that it may be the work of the great Sinan. The interior is grand and airy and the carved stone *mihrab* merits a look.

It would by a pity to leave Erzurum without paying a visit to the **Uç Kümbetler**, three mausolea down a lane on the right hand side of the Çifte Minareli Medresesi. No one seems to know precisely why they are here and who is buried in them but they have become one of the sights of the town and people like to pay a visit to them as they would to old friends. Children play here and lovers meet. They appear to date from the 13th–14th century and their presence and date show that the city had by then expanded beyond its walls.

PRACTICAL TIPS

GETTING THERE

By air: Erzurum airport (*T: 442 327 2835, www.erzurum.dhmi.gov.tr*), 11km west of town, has about half a dozen daily flights to and from Ankara, Istanbul and İzmir). The airport shuttle (*T: 442 243 0515*) leaves from near the train station. The journey takes approx. 30mins, depending on the traffic.
By bus: The *otogar*, 1km to the west of town, has bus services to a number of long-distance destinations, including Trabzon. The Gölbaşı Semt Garajı is a *dolmuş* station for locations north of Erzurum such as İspir, Yusufeli and the Çoruh Valley. They have a limited number of services; it might be a good idea to ask your hotel to ring and find out when the next *dolmuş* will depart. It is located to the east of town on Route 950, where it crosses the continuation of Ayazpaşa Cd. The *İlce otogar* marked on the map has local services for the Erzurum metropolitan area.
By train: There are trains to Erzincan and Divriği to the west (*described in the following chapter*), as well as to Kars to the east (*see Blue Guide Eastern Turkey*). But train journeys are very slow: it is only worth attempting if you have time to spare.
Tourist Information Office: Cemal Gürsel Cd 9/4 (*T: 442 218 5697*).

WHERE TO STAY

The Çağ Otel (*T: 442 235 5302, www.cagotel.com.tr*) between the railway station and the centre, on Millet Bahçe Cd, is neat and modern. At the Polat Otel (*T: 442 235 0363*) on Kazım Karabekir Cd near the Georgian Gate at the north end of town, rooms may a bit cramped but it has parking space and it is a cheaper choice. For a small budget, the Turkuaz Guesthouse (*T: 442 213 1321, www.turkuazbutikotel.tr.gg*) on İkikapılı Kahve Sk, behind the Garanti Bankası, has shared facilities on each of its three floors.

WHAT AND WHERE TO EAT

Cağ kebap is similar to a *döner kebap* but not identical. It is always made of lamb, not chicken, and is cooked on a horizontal spit. Delicious. You will find it at the **Güzelyurt**, a venerable place in business since 1928 (*Cumhuriyet Cd 42; T: 442 234 5001, www.guzelyurtrestaurant.com.tr*). **Vatan Lokantası**, near the Georgian Gate to the north of town, is another good choice.

LOCAL SPECIALITIES

James Morier described an interesting bazaar setting with shops tightly packed and accessed via staircases leading to the roof. The **Taşhan** near the Georgian Gate offers a somewhat tamer experience, but here you will find the *Oltu taşı*, the local speciality. It is a black stone not unlike jet, extensively used since the 18th century for prayer beads and now also for jewellery. Very soft when extracted, it is comparatively easy to work and hardens on contact with air. It is generally set in silver.

Erzincan, Divriği & Şebinkarahisar

MAMA HATUN KÜLLİYESİ

Between Erzurum and Erzincan, the **Mama Hatun Külliyesi**, 13km west of Tercan (*map C, 4*), is well worth a stop. It has been made ready for tourists with the help of an enthusiastic restoration programme, possibly financed by the treasure that, according to local lore, had been hidden in the caravanserai precisely for that purpose. Mama Hatun was a female ruler in a man's world. She was of the Saltukid family who ruled from Erzurum after the great breakthrough of the Battle of Manzikert in 1071. She herself is a legendary figure, very much part of Turkish folk literature. The complex includes her tomb, a caravanserai, a hamam and a bridge

The **mausoleum** is a clear departure from the standard, simpler *kümbet* of Iranian inspiration. This is a complex of tombs rather than a single one. The central kümbet, with eight lobes, the outside layout mirroring the inside arrangements, is an elegant construction topped by a fluted conical cap. It is surrounded by a tall wall accessed by an internal staircase. On the inside of the wall are eleven arches and niches presumed to be the resting places of relatives of Mama Hatun. The portal of the mausoleum is ornamented with fine cursive script in high relief. The name of the builder, Mufaddal the Cross-Eyed, who came from Ahlat, is inscribed there. The date is not given and one should not trust Evliya Çelebi, who was writing over four centuries later and made Mama Hatun into an Ak Koyunlu princess. Historical sources suggest that when a nephew of Saladin was preparing to invade the Ahlat region, beside Lake Van (*map D, 5*), she played a part in the operation, so a date somewhere in the late 12th or early 13th century is plausible. At that time Ahlat was an important artistic centre; Mama Hatun's mausoleum is therefore a precursor of (and also resembles) the Köşk Medrese built by the Emir Ertena's wife near Kayseri in 1339 to commemorate her husband. It has the same arcaded courtyard surrounding a kümbet. In spite of its name, its educational character is not proven.

The **caravanserai** of the Mama Hatun complex, bristling with chimney stacks, is of the standard plan with an inner courtyard and vast stabling arrangement for the mules, horses and camels of the caravans.

ERZİNCAN & ALTINTEPE

The road leads on to Erzincan (*map C, 4*), a place of very hot summers and freezing winters on the ancient trade routes to the east. The Urartians were the first settlers and they left their mark at Altıntepe (*see below*), but the area flourished under the Armenians, when the town, then known as Yerez, Eriza or Erez, was the centre of an important pre-Christian cult of the goddess Anahita. The temple, with its priests and hierodules (sacred prostitutes), has not been found. Its location was not within the walled town but in a village outside, protected by superstition as contemporary sources maintain. This did not stop the Roman general Antony from plundering it in the late 1st century BC (Pliny the Elder *32.82–3*). The cult was finally eradicated by Gregory the Illuminator some 300 years later.

ESKİ ERZİNCAN

Present day Erzincan, a friendly, bustling, commercial town, is recent: after the disastrous earthquake of 1939 the population moved to a new site 3km to the north. Eski Erzincan (Old Erzincan) was closer to the Euphrates, where it takes a turn southwest and carves its way through the Munzur Dağları. Remains are scant; the lines of the walls suggest it was some 150m by 200m, with a hexagonal tower. Evidence suggests, however, that the walls were no longer in use after the 16th century, when the town expanded and became the capital of an Ottoman province. The gatehouse, still inhabited after the 1939 earthquake, Ottoman in style, was built on top of medieval remains. Nineteenth-century travellers describe a wide arched doorway flanked by diminutive bastions. They also mention Kufic inscriptions and Christian sculptures. It is worth remembering that the city was on an international trade route and was famous—as Marco Polo testifies—for its soft white cotton cloth. In the 1320s, when the Mongols were ruling the town, Venice made an agreement with the Il Khan securing permission for a church and a Franciscan monastery.

ALTINTEPE

There are a number of places in Turkey that are called Altıntepe. 'Altın' is Turkish for gold, and the name usually indicated that treasure was found there. This Altıntepe (*map C, 4; open during daylight hours*), a few kilometres after Üzümlü, north of Erzincan, is no exception. A 1938 report speaks of an Urartian cauldron in an excellent state of preservation and other metal finds being unearthed by workers on the Sivas–Erzurum railway. Why they had to dig up a 60m-high volcanic hill surrounded by a plain is not explained, but illicit excavations had clearly been going on: when the first investigation took place in 1959–66 the site had already been damaged.

Altıntepe is a fortress very much in the Urartian style: a residence for the ruler; there is no known civilian settlement alongside it. The flat hilltop was enclosed by a wall with bastions. Within the wall stood the **temple** (presumably dedicated to Haldi, the main god of the Urartians), in a courtyard with wooden columns on carved stone bases. Inside the temple, whose entrance faced southeast, pedestals as well as a number of offerings, including carved ivories and elaborate metalwork, were found. The **hall**, on a higher level than the temple, also had columns, also on stone bases but made of mudbrick. Massive walls some 3m thick supported a flat roof. The fresco decoration, with sphinxes, sitting bulls, pomegranates and genii, has an Assyrian flavour. In its architecture and layout the complex has been compared to the 8th-century fortress in Erebuny, overlooking Yerevan in modern-day Armenia, which was built by Argisti I. New excavations from 2003 have concentrated on the **burials** on the slopes. These were either hewn in the rock or constructed in masonry with corbelled roofs and niches, and closed by stone slabs. A number of sarcophagi and metal offerings were retrieved. The basalt stelae and libation basins found outside were part of open-air cult activities.

There are no signs of violent destruction, as is the case with so many Urartian fortresses. This one was seemingly abandoned, though that did not mean the end of the life of the site. During the latest excavations a fine mosaic floor with animal motifs, from a 6th-century **Byzantine basilica**, was exposed. The most recent layers of the hill are medieval.

KEMAH & DİVRİĞİ

On the way to Divriği, the flat-topped hill of **Kemah Kalesi** (*map C, 4*), protected on two sides by the Euphrates and one of its tributaries, looks ideal for a fortress—and indeed that is exactly what it was. It began as an Armenian principality and some members of the Arsacid Armenian dynasty (1st–5th centuries) were buried here. It also had a temple dedicated to the pagan goddess Anahita, suppressed by Gregory the Illuminator in his Christian zeal. Kemah came to prominence under the Byzantines, as it was on the border with the conquering Arabs. The 80m-high plateau was extensively fortified and the whole town, now sprawling in the plain, nestled within the walls. Tunnels were bored, cisterns were dug. These measures did not make it impregnable forever. The Arabs failed in their siege of 766, but in the 14th century Timur successfully stormed it after filling the river gorge with logs. Kemah was later used by the Ottomans in their tussles with local warlords. The citadel was finally abandoned in the 19th century.

The principal attraction at Kemah today are the stunning views. The line of the citadel walls can be followed; the circuit is cut in half in the middle by an extra line of defences. Recent excavations by a Turkish team have identified a number of Ottoman buildings and retrieved a bundle of 198 pages of 16th-century manuscripts and lithographs, including a Qur'an, from the remains of a hamam near the mosque.

DİVRİĞİ

Situated high on the Çaltı Su, a tributary of the Euphrates, the town of Divriği (*map C, 3*) developed on a west-facing slope and on the valley floor; it is backed by the steep citadel mound overlooking a narrow gorge. In antiquity it was on an important road, as the Roman legionaries on their way to *Satala* (*see p. 35*) from *Melitene* (Malatya) crossed the Çaltı Su, thus avoiding thus the Euphrates. Otherwise Divriği remains difficult to explain, its extraordinary monuments all the more so. It probably had a defensive function; more importantly though, it was a refuge beyond the reach of central authority. Certainly it was that which drove the Paulician Armenians here in the mid-9th century; it is no coincidence that today it has a large Alevi population.

HISTORY OF DİVRİĞİ

When the Paulicians took refuge here, the town was known as *Tephrike*. The Paulicians take their name from Bishop Paul of Antioch, whose teachings they followed. They were deemed heretical as they did not adopt the mainstream Christian doctrine of rejecting the Old Testament and venerating Mary, Mother of God, preferring instead a system of dualistic doctrines possibly inspired by Manicheism, and objecting to any form of ecclesiastical hierarchy. They were encouraged by the Arabs as a suitable diversion to keep the Byzantines occupied. The Emir of Melitene cast a favourable eye on the setting up of a principality at Tephrike by Karbeas, the Paulician leader, in 843. The Paulicians then joined forces with the Arabs in raids on Byzantine lands.

The Byzantines eventually captured Tephrike, and after a spell in Armenian hands, it fell to the Seljuks after 1071.

WHAT TO SEE IN DİVRİĞİ

The town is well worth a visit: one can admire its **fine wooden houses** and watch the metalworkers hammering away. The remains of the fortifications on the **citadel** (walls and polygonal towers) are mainly 13th-century, rebuilt after the Mongol raids on earlier Byzantine foundations. They are best visited for the view of the town, of the steep gorge and of Kesdoğan Kale on the other side of the river. The castle mosque may date from 1180, though it has been thoroughly rebuilt (*normally closed*). The town used to be contained within the circuit of walls but has since spilled out onto the sunny slopes beyond them.

The **Great Mosque and Hospital** (*open Tues–Sat 8–5*), now justly on UNESCO's World Heritage List, are a single building on a platform overlooking the town. They are the work of Khurramshad, an architect from Ahlat, the leading artistic centre at the time (*see Blue Guide Eastern Turkey*). They date to c. 1228 and have been recently beautifully restored after a period of abandonment. It is not usual for Muslims to abandon mosques, but this is Alevi country and the Alevis do not use mosques, worshipping instead in a *cemevi* (assembly house): this one became a stables in the 1900s before being abandoned. The building dates from a time when the Seljuks were the overlords and the local principality was run by the Mengujekids, loyal subordinate rulers. The mosque was willed by Ahmet Shah and the hospital by his wife, Turan Malik. It is very grand for such a small place and does not reflect a sudden period of prosperity: it is a one off, a pure act of piety. Divriği is not a particularly rich place. There are iron mines, it is true, but even they are not enough to explain anything on this scale.

The **hospital**, a *marestan* or hospice for the insane, is on the south side of the complex. Its two-storey portal is particularly noticeable for its delicate and elaborate carving, contrasting with the stark plainness of the walls on either side. In the interior, beyond a vestibule, steps lead to small upstairs rooms along the south side. Downstairs the space is open, with three *iwans* and a pool in the middle with a spiral run-off. The only source of light is the oculus above. The northeast room communicating with the mosque houses three tombs and fine faïence décor.

The **mosque** had two main entrances (the one to the east, now a window, was apparently part of the original plan). The style of the west portal, with lotus flowers, fleurs de lys, squares and triangles, was seemingly inspired by Armenian manuscript decoration; it is not Seljuk (it has been compared to architectural elements from Rum Kale; *see Blue Guide Southeastern Turkey*). The north portal is the most elaborate, though according to some, while it displays great skill, it lacks unity, displaying a juxtaposition of discordant elements. There are no empty surfaces and its decoration is perhaps too crowded. The carving is deep and imitates stucco. The effect is not helped by the fact that the space in front is limited and there is nowhere to take it all in from a good perspective. Inside, the stone ceiling is supported by a forest of columns. The only source of light is the oculus, so the light is rather dim—but very suggestive. The south end has a dome with an intricately carved mihrab below it. The wooden minbar, dated 1240, is also a fine piece of woodwork. According to T.A. Sinclair, the plan of the mosque is of Iranian inspiration. It encloses a courtyard which is reduced to a mere oculus; the axis is north–south. It is a departure from the standard pattern of a mosque with a prayer hall and separate courtyard, which is found south of the Taurus Mountains, in Diyarbakır for instance.

Divriği also had a reputation for its **cats**, at least according to Evliya Çelebi (though it is unwise to believe everything he says). In the accounts of his travels he talks about the plight of the cats at Ardabil, a town in Persia close to the Caspian Sea. Here the mice were terrible, nibbling at anything from cloaks to moustaches. The cats had short lives and so a trade developed from Divriği, or so he maintains. The Divriği cats, fat and sturdy and trained to hunt, found great favour in Ardabil. The cat brokers loved them and proudly paraded them for sale on their heads—as cat sellers still do in Istanbul. There is also a darker side to this tale. Because of the varied hues of their coats and the quality of their fur, the very same Divriği cats fed a lively trade in cat fur garments. It is said that the quality rivalled squirrel pelts from Muscovy.

ŞEBİNKARAHİSAR

Şebinkarahisar (*map C, 4*) sits in the broad valley of the Büyük Irmak, just over 100km south of Giresun in the shadow of an isolated dark rock, which explains why it was called *Maurokastron* (by the Genoese and the Greeks) and *Karahisar* (by the Turks); both names mean 'Black Castle'. The first part of the name (*şebin*) refers to the alum mines in the vicinity. The town started as a veteran colony founded by Pompey after his defeat of Mithridates VI. It is possible, though, that beneath the castle on the black rock lurks a Pontic fortress. The elevation provides a natural refuge, an impregnable stronghold; it dominates the valley. As such it was used by the Paulicians (*see p. 49*) and much later by the Armenians, when they made their tragic last stand against the Ottoman troops in 1915. The Byzantines held it for a while but it was already lost to the Turkmen soon after the battle of Manzikert. Its economy, however, remained in foreign hands (Genoese and Greek) right up until the 19th century, well after the Ottoman conquest. It was based on the alum mines.

ALUM MINING

Ever since antiquity the use of alum as an astringent, water purifier and an indispensable compound for dyeing, fulling and tanning has been well known. It was found in small quantities in Spain, Morocco, Egypt and on the islands of Vulcano and Ischia in the Tyrrhenian Sea. The exploitation of the mines at Şebinkarahisar appears to have started in the early 13th century (though one does wonder if there was any previous Roman involvement, despite the lack of conclusive evidence). It peaked in the 12th–14th centuries. The two main challeges were the supply of workers and the organisation of transport. The mining works were in the hands of the Greeks, either directly from Trabzon and its the hinterland, or indirectly from Gümüşhane, when workers is the silver mines there were laid off. Transport was in the hands of Genoese traders. The preferred route was via Sivas and Phocaea to the Aegean, or via Trabzon and, occasionally, over the mountains, to Giresun, depending on the political situation. The exploitation of the mines continued into Ottoman times (the mines had been assigned to the Ottoman treasury but were still run by the Greek *archimetallurgoi*; the Genoese had long departed) and lasted on and off until the 19th century, though Şebinkarahisar had long lost its supremacy by then. Around 1460 a new abundant source of excellent quality alum had been found in Italy, in the Tolfa region north of Rome, which at that time was part of the Papal States. Pope Pius II hit on the idea of using this windfall to finance his wars against the Turks by setting up a Cassa della Crociata (literally a 'crusade bank') and running the trade as a monopoly, constraining all of Christendom to purchase alum from the papacy. The plan was doomed to failure: Venice was never compliant in the scheme and alum was soon discovered elsewhere, in Spain and on the Isle of Wight.

THE CASTLE

The castle has a citadel with a pentagonal dungeon and a keep with inner steps to the top on its highest point. It is surrounded by a wall, 1km long, with towers at the corners and a four-storey tower in the wall opposite the gate. The walls are thick and of fine ashlar construction. The town was never meant to be confined within the enceinte; it may be that the medieval town is under the present settlement on the slope. In the castle a number of rock-cut stairs lead to tunnels and to cisterns, a feature typical of Pontic fortresses. The present state of the building is the result of many reworkings, from Byzantine to Ottoman to recent restorations.

NİKSAR

Heading west down the valley of the Kelkit, Niksar (*map C, 1*) is the next Pontic fortress. It could well be Cabeira, the favourite residence of Mithridates VI (*Strabo 12.3.30*), the place where he kept his valuables. Not much is left of it. Nor is there much left of ancient *Neocaesarea*, the name given it by the Romans when they refounded the town. Wars and earthquakes have taken their toll but the valley that the city commands, the ancient *Phanaroia*, is still incredibly fertile. Oil and wine have now given way to other forms of cultivation but the rich pastures are still put to the same use as in antiquity.

The only surviving remains are on the acropolis, a slim rock between two valleys at the edge of the plain overlooking the town from the east. The present ruins (a fair amount of the building stone has been reused in the town) are Turkish, on Roman substructures. Some scholars would like to believe that the Temple of Men Pharnakes was here but recent analysis disagrees (*see Temple States, below*). Nevertheless, ritual certainly had its place in the fortress, with animal sacrifices being performed—as Gregory the Illuminator found out when he came here. However, it seems that he turned a blind eye to such goings on, electing to reclothe the practice as a commemoration of martyrs.

An interesting monument in the northwest corner of the Kale is the **Nizameddin Yağıbasan medresesi**, one of the earliest in Anatolia, built in 1157–8 by the Danishmendid rulers of Sivas. The building has a complex history, having also served at some point as a church. Forever being rebuilt, it is now undergoing yet another restoration programme; the present medrese probably retains little of the original. But the view is unchanged. It is tempting to wonder whom the church was for: perhaps for Bohemond of Antioch, one of the leaders of the First Crusade, who was imprisoned here in 1101.

TEMPLE STATES

The countryside between Zile, Niksar and Tokat was, in antiquity, under the special administrative jurisdiction of the Temple State. Temple states are broadly speaking religious entities with an economic basis that ensures their independence. There are geographical and chronological variations to the different regimes and such systems are also known in ancient Mesopotamia and Egypt. Here in the heart of Pontus, inland where it joins the Anatolian plateau, the development is Hellenistic; some have attempted to trace it to the Hittites, who had a temple in the area, but the connection is tentative and the evidence poor. Indeed the only real evidence here is Strabo, who was writing in the Roman period but who had the advantage of being a local and of having a relative who had earlier been appointed to the highest position in the administration. There is little information about the Mithridatic era. It appears, on the whole, that with the transition to Roman rule, the high priest, now appointed by the emperor in Rome, was not as powerful as when he had been appointed by the King of Pontus and was entitled to wear a diadem.

Apart from the priests there were the sacred slaves (hierodules), indispensable for working the land (the third element of a temple state) but the priest's power over them was not absolute. They belonged to the temple, not to the priest, and they could not be sold. Sacred prostitutes also had a role to play. Strabo makes a moralistic comment on the topic (*12.3.36*). His comparison to Corinth, which had been destroyed by the Romans well over a 100 years earlier, shows that he was writing for effect, forgetting that prostitution is the 'oldest profession'.

There were three main centres: Comana, Zela and Ameira. **Comana Pontica** (*map C, 3*) is by far the best known. It is situated along the Yeşilırmak river (the ancient *Iris*) on a site now bordered by routes 850 and 180. The river provided communication with Armenia Minor to the east and Amasya to the west. This made Comana a trading as well as a religious centre, with twice-yearly extravagant festivals. Its territory, a depressed valley bottom filled with very good soil, was tilled by 6,000 slaves. The site was identified on the hill of Hamamtepe in the mid-1800s, thanks to architectural elements found there and also to a number of inscribed blocks reused in the Roman bridge over the Yeşilırmak and now embedded in a concrete water regulator. Surveys have concluded that although the site covered a much larger area than just the hill of Hamamtepe, the Temple of Ma is probably up there. Excavations began in 2010 and have uncovered Seljuk and Byzantine levels. The temple, if and when it is found, is exepcted to be tetrastyle, as it appears on the coinage. The date of the goddess Ma's appearance in Anatolia is unknown. Some have seen her as a mother goddess, like the one worshipped at Pessinus, but attributes in the iconography suggest a female warrior. She bore the epithets 'invincible' and 'goddess of victory' and is represented with a spear and a shield, which suggests a precursor of Bellona (the Greek Enyo), goddess of war.

Zela now Zile (*map C, 3*) is due west of Tokat. The temple and the land here were sacred to Anahita, a Persian goddess introduced in the area around the 6th century BC. The Achaemenids built a temple here in the 4th century BC which was possibly developed later by the Pontic kings. A goddess of water and fertility also worshipped by the Armenians, Anahita was held in great veneration by the Pontic people. After the Roman conquest, Zela acquired urban status with an enlarged territory and new buildings. A theatre, partly carved out of the rock on which the temple stood, was built in stone and wood; the temple itself, according to Roman imperial coinage, was hexastyle. A great festival, in which the men dressed up as Scythians and spent the night feasting with their women and celebrating a victory of Cyrus the Great over the Scythians, was held every year. Under the Romans, Zela lost its independence: it is likely that Pompey wanted to rid the region once and for all of Persian influence. A three-word dispatch issued from Zela has lasted longer than the temple. When Caesar left Cleopatra after wintering in Egypt in 47 BC, he came this way to put an end to the simmering troubles in the region. His campaign was only five days long and his description of it (*'Veni,* *vidi, vici!*') appropriately terse. He penned it in a letter to a friend, but soon it had made the rounds in Rome. Eventually it was displayed in the triumphal parade through the Eternal City.

The **Temple of Men Pharnakes at Ameira** has not been securely located. It was probably near Niksar (*see above*) in the Phanaroia, a very fertile region, covered in vines and olives in antiquity and now given over to fruit, tobacco, opium and rice. This was a key site for the Pontic kings. Here they took their sacred oath: 'by the Fortune of the King and by Men Pharnakes'. Men Pharnakes may have a Hittite past as a moon god and probably came from Persia, where the Mithridatic dynasty had family connections (the founder of the Pharnacids, Pharnaces, a nobleman of the Persian Empire, had married the sister of Cyrus II).

With the advent of Roman rule, only Comana retained its special status. Although it came under imperial jurisdiction, it remained sacred and acquired the right of asylum. It lasted as a separate administrative unit until it became indefensible and people moved to the safety of Tokat (*described in the following chapter*). With the *Pax Ottomana*, the land reverted to its special status as a private domain of the *Valide Sultan*. The other two temple states may have been suppressed because of Pompey's decision to create a network of cities to administer the land and his desire to break the Persian connection.

PRACTICAL TIPS

GETTING THERE

By bus: Şebinkarahisar and Niksar are both off the main thoroughfare, the E80 (Route 100). Any bus that runs between Erzurum and Samsun will get you there. You will need to get off at Suşehri for Şebinkarahisar and at the junction with Route 850 for Niksar. Divriği's small bus station is in the centre of town and offers services that will get you to the main trunk roads, from where you can board a long-distance bus.

By train: Divriği is on the train line from Erzurum to Sivas; if you can spare the time (train journeys in Turkey are slow), it is well worth it.

WHERE TO STAY

At **Şebinkarahisar** the Hancilar Hotel (*T: 454 711 3540*) is in the old town directly below the Kale and offers good value for money. The Başaran Otel (*T: 454 711 4320*), on the main Cumhuriyet Cd, is also an inexpensive choice.

In **Divriği** the Divriği Belediyesi Misafirhanesi (*T: 346 418 1825, www.divrigi.bel.tr*) is a very good and a reasonably-priced choice. It is close to the station on the north side of the railway track with a fine view over the Kale (especially handy if you arrive by train in the middle of the night).

Thirteen kilometres north of Niksar, on the road to Ünye at the **Ardıçlı Dağ**

Evi (*open 1st June–26th Sept; T 356 542 1242, www.kucukvebutikoteller.com/ardicli-dag-evi-niksar*), Şehsuvar and Nevber Savuran run two chalets in the middle of the woods. Excellent if you want to take time off and are not looking for budget accommodation. Meals are available on location; some shared facilities.

WHERE TO EAT

Near the Başaran Otel in **Şebinkarahisar**, the Çiğköftecim Lokanta is run (unusually) by a mother and middle-aged daughter team. Try the excellent *lahmacun*, a flat dough topped with mincemeat (lamb or beef) and chopped vegetables that remains very flexible after baking. It is normally eaten rolled up with a garnish of raw vegetables, onions and parsley inside and accompanied with a glass of cool *ayran* to counteract the pepper.

Sivas, Tokat & Amasya

SİVAS

Sivas (*map C, 3*) sits close to the Kızılırmak river (the *Marassantiya* of the Hittites), before it takes the plunge south and makes its great sweep, eventually discharging quantities of red sediment (hence its name, *kızıl* means 'red') into the Black Sea in a swampy delta. In Sivas the river opens up and roads meet in the valley. Sivas has always been a place of commercial and military importance. People were not put off by the severe climate: Sivas's winters, when the rivers freeze and icy winds blow, are notorious.

HISTORY OF SİVAS

There is a mound at the south end of town now topped by a tea house: excavations show a sequence from Classical to Ottoman; Pompey's Megalopolis may have been here. The new foundation was part of the Roman strategy of setting up a network of cities, administrative centres on the Greek model. Not long after it became Sebaste. There are a number of cities in Asia Minor whose names are a variation on *Sevastos*, a Greek term meaning 'worthy of respect'.

Nothing much is left of Sivas's Classical past—few inscriptions, no sculptures—but the memory of its martyrs lingers on. The **Forty Martyrs of Sebasteia**, soldiers of the *Legio XII Fulminata* who refused to abjure their faith and died of exposure in early March 320, indicate that the town was surrounded by icy marshes—in which the martyrs were forced to stand through the night. The story of St Blaise, the first bishop of Sebaste, who tended the wild animals pursued by the emperor's hunters, suggests that somewhere there must have been an amphitheatre, to which the captured creatures were taken for *venationes*. The presence of a bishop also indicates a sizeable Christian community in the early days of the 4th century.

Sebaste's great advantage, its ease of communication, was probably also its main weakness, since it made it an easy and crucial target. Justinian restored its defences but as the situation deteriorated, Sebaste was contested by the Arabs and the Seljuks, and also enjoyed the dubious privilege of being sacked by a Byzantine emperor, Romanos IV, in 1068. By the 13th century it had settled down under the Seljuks as a prosperous trading station with links to Mesopotamia and Iran. The Genoese did not miss their opportunity. They had an outpost here to control the alum trade (*see p. 51*) from Şebinkarahisar to Phocaea. The city walls were rebuilt and the monuments for which Sivas is justly famous went up. But destruction was to come. Timur sacked it in 1402, in retaliation for its surrender to the Ottomans. The remanants that were left were contested by the Mamluks and by local *derebeys*. The population, a mix of Armenians, Greek Orthodox and Alevi Muslims, must have been happy to find some peace under the Ottomans, even though it meant a genteel decline as trade routes shifted. The east–west route did not recover until the 1900s.

In September 1919 the Sivas Congress was held here, in the Boys' School, a rare stone building built in 1892 (most buildings in town were then of mud brick). Presiding over the conference was Mutafa Kemal, later Atatürk, with delegates from all the Anatolian provinces of the Ottoman Empire. It marked one of the turning points in giving the war of independence a national character. The building now houses the **Ethnographic Museum** (*open Tues–Sun 8.30–12 & 1–5*).

EXPLORING THE TOWN

The **Gök Medrese** (*map Sivas*) looks forlorn and out of place on the south edge of town. It takes its name from the blue tiles of its elegant decoration, particularly that of the north *iwan*. It was willed by Sahip Ata Fahrettin Ali in 1271, when he was in charge of the Sultanate of Rum (he also had a medrese built in Kayseri and a mosque in Konya). The architect was Armenian. It was a museum in 1926; restoration and rebuilding works have been in progress since 1979 and are still not complete. The building will eventually become part of the local university. The impressive portal, flanked by two minarets (accessed from the inside north room), is decorated with intricate work in carved stone, brick tiles and marble. The two-storey courtyard is arcaded with three *iwans*. The columns are Byzantine. The decoration in the courtyard is a continuous line of floral motifs around the top of the ground floor. It is reminiscent of the ornamentation of the Buruciye Medresesi (*see below*).

The other main monuments in Sivas (all accessible) stand in what is technically a park (Selçuk Parkı; *map Sivas*), though the trees have been felled. It's an unwelcoming, hot expanse of paving stones dotted with unexplained archaeology above ground and below, under glass. Fortunately the **Buruciye Medresesi**, at the north end of the park, is now a bazaar and one can always take shelter in its welcoming shade. The Muzaffer Buruciye Medresesi, to give it its full name, dates roughly to 1271/2 and was offered to the town by a private individual. He was born in Burijird in Persia, hence the name. The entrance portal and niches are elaborate. Beyond is an arcaded courtyard with three *iwans* and Classical and Byzantine columns. To the left is the burial chamber of the donor. His name is mentioned in the inscription that runs all around the room, in elegant characters on fine blue and turquoise tiles. The light may be dim, but that adds to the truly suggestive atmosphere. The room with the brick dome at the other side of the entrance was a prayer room and is now a shop.

Of the nearby **Çifte Minareli Medrese**, only the façade is left. It was established by the Mongol governor in 1271 as a school for the study of the Qur'an and the sayings of the Prophet. It has been in a parlous state for some time and used to have a modern school built up against it at the back; in 1882 it was a hospital. Excavations have shown that it had two storeys with four *iwans* and a courtyard.

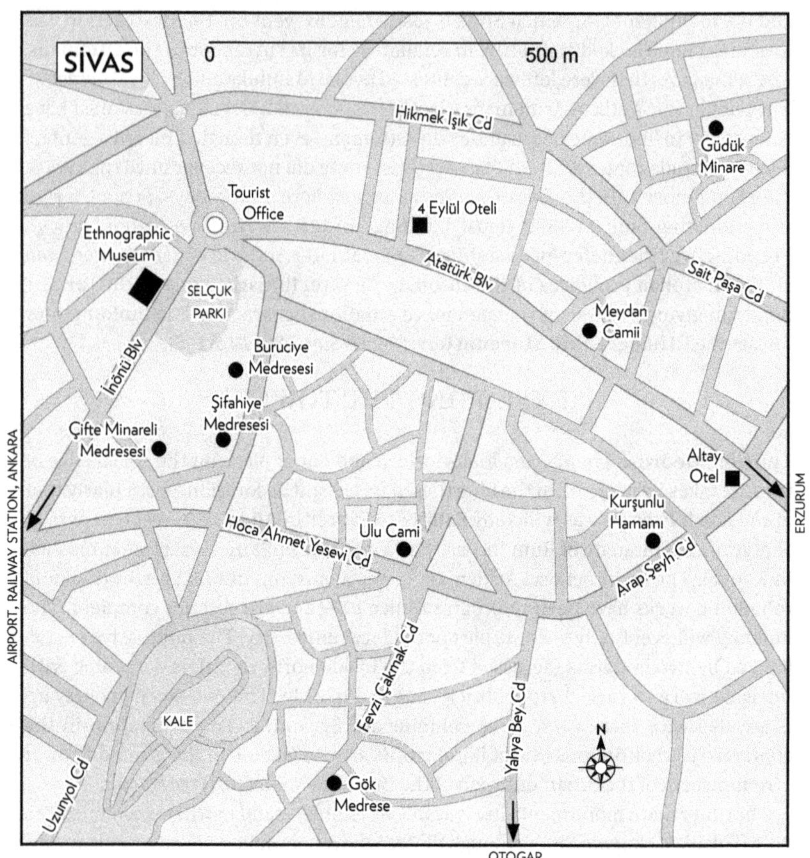

The hospital of Kay Kavus, also known as **Şifahiye Medresesi** (now a café and bazaar), was founded by the Seljuk sultan of that name in 1217–18 and houses his tomb. Beyond the portal, the deep entrance hall leads to a single-storey courtyard with arcades and cells. The plan is that of a medrese. The *iwan* at the east end has human heads on the arch, which have been interpreted as the sun and the moon. The *türbe* of the founder is on the south side of the building and is decorated with glazed and unglazed bricks. Interestingly the charitable deeds of the endowment of the foundation contain details of the medical and surgical procedures carried out in the building.

The 14th-century **Güdük Minare** is a *türbe* that has lost its conical cap; it is truncated, as the name *güdük* indicates. The square stone base melts into an arrangement of triangles framed by bricks and emerges as a circular drum. The remains of the deceased, Şeyh Hasan Bey, son of Eretna, a Mongol officer who ruled Anatolia after the Il Khanate, are in a black marble sarcophagus in the tomb chamber.

SULUSARAY & HOROZTEPE

The road out of Sivas to the north climbs over the pass and descends into the valley of the Yeşilırmak, another of those twisting Pontic rivers. The *Iris* of Classical times, it flows through Tokat and the famed Dazimonitis Plain (*see below*). You are approaching the heart of Pontus here, at Amasya. On the way to Tokat, if you are not in a hurry, take a turning left to Artova off Route 850 after the Çamlıbel Geçidi pass and continue to **Sulusaray**. It is a fine drive that has to be taken slowly to admire the countryside and the valley of the Çekerek river. Here is the site of the town of *Sebastopolis*, a Hellenistic or Roman foundation already in decline by the time of the Byzantines. Recent excavations (in 2013) have added to the clutch of previous finds, mainly architectural elements and inscriptions. The baths fed by thermal springs 3km away, as well as a circular temple and a Byzantine church, have been exposed.

East of Route 850, just before Tokat at the site of **Horoztepe**, illegal excavations in the 1950s brought to light a number of extraordinary bronzes from an Early Bronze Age cemetery. Some are in Ankara's Museum of Civilisations, others found their way through art dealers to the Metropolitan Museum in New York and to other American institutions.

TOKAT

Tokat (*map C, 3*) is a comparatively new town in a very ancient landscape. It is a pretty place on a branch of the Yeşilırmak, the Tokat Su, which crosses it north–south. Around it, in the **Dazimonitis Plain** (now Kazovası, the 'Plain of the Geese') and in the adjacent lands, temple states (*see p. 52*) developed, and the Mithridatic dynasty took its chances here after the fall of the Persian Empire at the hands of Alexander the Great in the 4th century BC. The kingdom's heartland was at Amasya (*described below*), but the rock-cut tunnels and stairs so characteristic of Mithridatic fortresses are all over the place and the memory has not faded.

Tokat as a town is first mentioned in the 4th century AD and it develops from this time, as paganism is supplanted by the new religion. The land around it, the fertile Dazimonitis, remained administratively separate. The Byzantines built the first fortress on the Kale (unless Mithridates got there first, but it is probably too late now for an investigation). They were followed by the Seljuks. The town was contested by the Ak Koyunlu chief Uzun Hasan, and then settled down to a period of prosperity, weaving silk, dyeing and printing cloth and processing raw materials from Anatolia. Trade was in the hands of the Armenians and the Greeks, though two thirds of the population was Muslim. Towards the end of the 19th century Tokat benefited handsomely from the redeveloped port of Samsun. The Greek population doubled: in 1905 there were five Greek schools in town.

EXPLORING TOKAT

The most interesting part of town is around **Tokat Kalesi**, which is high up and cannot be missed. The citadel sits on two peaks, with the southeast side being the most precipitous. There may easily have been a refuge fortress here, as the rock provided safety when the people in the broad open plain below felt threatened. Whatever its past, Tokat Kalesi has now been completely rebuilt in one single style; mercifully over time the stark white hue of the new stone has mellowed. It is worth climbing the zig-zag route up the north slope past an old part of town that has maintained its character. The Kale has had an interesting life, doubling up as a prison for high-status captives, including a number of Frenchmen who had fought for Muhammed Ali when he rebelled against the Ottomans in Egypt in the 19th century; they left some graffiti. From the Kale there is a good view of the old town, which stretches west up the side valley and is well worth a relaxed walk for the chance to see some **domestic Ottoman architecture**.

Other sights are in the eastern part of town along the Tokat Su. The **Taşhan** (or Voyvada Han), a 17th-century building, is open for business (with tourist shops) and for coffee. The **Hatuniye Medresesi and Camii** were built by Bayezıt II in memory of his wife Maria de Doubera (*see p. 16*); note the portico at the entrance and its fine Classical columns strengthened by double and triple bronze rings and supporting capitals in various styles.

The **museum** (*open Tues–Sun 8.30–5*), with the usual assortment of sarcophagi, ceramics, stelae, coins and interesting ethnographic material, is in the Gök Medrese (its name means 'sky blue', though its portal is in fact red). Originally a theological school and hospital, it was restored and redesigned in 1982.

The **Latifoğlu Konağı** (*officially open Tues–Sun 8.30–5*) affords a glimpse into 19th-century-style interior decoration. The Seljuk bridge over the Yeşilırmak, the **Hıdırlık Köprüsü** with its five-pointed arches, is in the north part of town roughly on the continuation of Gazi Osman Paşa Blv.

AROUND TOKAT

On the way to Amasya you can take a detour to Pazar off Route 180 to the south for the **Ballıca Mağarası** caves (*signed; open daylight hours; charge*). They are very extensive and photogenic. The air is said to be excellent for asthmatics and for dwarf bats, who live here in droves. On the way back, have a look by the Seljuk bridge at the mid-12th-century **Mahperi Hatun Kervansaray**, now restored and turned into a restaurant. It has fine vaulted rooms and a large hall. At **Turhal** there is not much to see apart from a fine view. The inevitable ruined Pontic Kale stands at the highest point. Is this Strabo's *Gaziura* (*12.3.15*)?

AMASYA

Amasya (*map C, 1*) sits in a very picturesque setting in the valley of the Yeşilırmak, where it narrows into a defile. Ogier Ghiselin de Busbecq, ambassador to Suleyman the Magnificent c. 1555 and responsible, among other things, for introducing tulips to Holland, was very taken with it and compared it to a theatre with a wonderful view.

With its 300m rock, the Harşena Dağı, providing a strong defensive position and the proximity of the river, it is possible that occupation dates back very early indeed. But Amasya is in an earthquake zone and has been poorly investigated. Much remains to be done. The city came to prominence when the Mithridatic dynasty used it as its capital from 280–180 BC. It was then *Amaseia*. The dynasty, of Persian origin, carved out a kingdom for itself here at the time of the dissolution of the Persian Empire in the turmoil following the conquests of Alexander the Great. In the earlier 4th century BC they were the rulers of the town of Chios in Mysia to the west. Mithridates Ktistes (the 'Builder'), founder of the dynasty, was a vassal of Antigonos Monophalmos, a Macedonian satrap who for a time ruled Asia Minor. Mithridates Ktistes fled to Paphlagonia c. 301 BC in fear for his life when his loyalty came under suspicion. He had few followers but slowly and steadily built up his dominion and c. 281 BC declared himself king. The kingdom expanded over time, with his successors occupying large tracts of Asia Minor and almost the complete circuit of the Black Sea. The realm was eventually conquered by the Romans, in 63 BC. Because of the defensive position of the fortress, the Byzantines, Arabs, Mongols and Ottomans have all fought for it, so there is not much left. With the Ottomans came some respite and a new name, Amasya. The town became a centre of culture and learning, the 'Baghdad of Rum' (the 'Oxford of Anatolia' title is later, from the mid-19th century). Fires and earthquakes later diminished its importance and Amasya is now well established in its role as a provincial capital and a producer of famous apples and pears. The wine for which it was renowned in antiquity is now, unfortunately, a distant memory.

IN AND AROUND THE KALE

In Amasya the interesting part is the **Kale** and the area immediately fronting it. Here the houses, reflected in the placid Yeşilırmak, make a fine view: one is reminded of the well-known Miroir d'Ornans near Besançon in France. The area was walled in antiquity and remains of a Hellenistic circuit can be seen on the slopes of the **acropolis**. This is the place described by Strabo when he talks of the monuments of his native city (*12.3.39*). Of the residence of the Pontic kings, not much that is original remains; what one sees on the hill today is a modern reconstruction, apart from three tunnels, one of which accessed the spring that supplied water to the royal residence. It is thought that the derelict Kızlar Saray, halfway up the slope, lies over the remains of an older building. The present structures, if one can judge from the name, probably belonged to an Ottoman harem.

The **tombs of the Pontic kings** were only properly investigated in 2002. By then, unsurprisingly, they were empty, but careful examination of the remains by a German team has produced interesting results. They are Hellenistic in date and they follow on from a long tradition of rock tombs in Anatolia, dating back to the Urartians. The tombs are five in all. Starting from the east, next to the well-preserved Hellenistic wall, are three tombs; a group of two is situated to the west.

They are accessed by staircases cut in the rock and the two groups are connected by tunnels. At the time of their construction they were intended to be free-standing, with a corridor going all around, but only in three are the corridors complete. In one case it seems that the rock proved to be unstable and work came to a halt. Otherwise it is possible that work was interrupted in the early 2nd century BC, when King Pharnakes I decided to move his capital to Sinop. All the chambers have a high entrance, only accessible with a ladder. This is a Persian feature, expressing a concern with purity. Similar high entrances are found at Persepolis. All the chambers are small; they were meant for a limited number of people. Careful examination shows that three tombs had fronts with four to six columns in the style of a Greek temple. Additional and separate architectural elements, such as stone revetment and thresholds, were secured with clamps and dowels, the locations of which are still apparent. The sequence of construction is not a linear progression towards a full Greek appearance, as is the case in other tomb groups in Anatolia. On the contrary, here the earlier tombs are very much inspired by Greek temple architecture, while the most recent one, built for Pharnakes, is as un-Greek as possible with its barrel-vaulted shape. Pharnakes was never laid to rest in it; he had moved his capital to Sinop, where neither his burial place nor that of later kings (probably in the form of a tumulus or a mausoleum) have been located. To visit the tombs, cross the river by the bridge fronting the steps that leads to them. Do look under the bridge to see how it is supported: arches topped by pilasters, and not the other way round as one would expect. The ascent to the castle is via a signposted road. The ruins have been made to look as new, but the view is still worth it.

MONUMENTS IN TOWN

Back in town there are a number of monuments, mainly of Ottoman date. The **Bimarhane** (*closed Mon*), on the main thoroughfare, has recently been restored and can be admired while sipping a drink. It is a truly magnificent building with fine carvings, the only building left from the Mongol period (it is dated 1308). Originally a mental hospital, it was built by the Il Khan Öljeitü for his wife Yıldız Hatun.

The **Sultan Beyazıt Külliyesi**, close to the river, is a grand complex set in cool greenery and built in 1486; it is now unfortunately squeezed between two busy roads. Parts of it are still in use so it may not be possible to visit all the building, but do enjoy the shade. It was built by Sultan Beyazıt's son Şehzade Ahmet, when he was governor of Amasya. He never became sultan because he was killed by his brother Selim. The **archaeological museum** nearby (*open Tues–Sun 9.30–5; charge*) has the usual array of local finds and, as a diversion, a display of seven local mummies (the only Muslim mummies in the world), preserved by a process of natural mummification thanks to the sealed micro-environment.

The Taşhan (late 17th-century market) by the **Burmalı Minare Camii** has been restored. The mosque (mid-13th-century Seljuk) is not particularly attractive but the spiral minaret has style. The **Sokullu Mehmet Paşa Cami ve Çeşmesi** is built right against the rock. It dates to 1486 and was commissioned by Lala Mehmet Paşa, tutor to the son of Sultan Beyazıt II. Note the elegant porch and the intricately decorated *mimber*.

Finally, while the castle had its own water supply (tunnelled from the acropolis; *see above*), the town itself might have relied on the river. As Evliya Çelebi bluntly put it, 'Tokat dumps it and Amasya drinks it.' This problem must have been noted in antiquity since Amasya had its own **aqueduct**, the remains of which, cut in the rock, can be seen in places on the right bank of the river along the road from Tokat. Nearer town the valley widens and the aqueduct continued on conventional arches, of which nothing remains. A 3rd-century AD inscription mentioning aqueduct repairs has been built into a nearby mosque. Today the aqueduct has entered local lore: if you ask anyone, they will tell you it was built by Ferhat to impress his beloved Şirin. Details on when he drove a tunnel through the mountains are scarce, but the lovers have their monument on the river front and their museum (**Ferhat ile Şirin Aşıkler Müzesi**) at the beginning of the tunnel on the right-hand side of the road as you come from Tokat.

PRACTICAL TIPS

GETTING THERE

By air: Sivas, Tokat and Amasya all have airports with connections to Istanbul. The airports are some distance out of town and are accessible by taxi or private transport.
By train: Sivas and Amasya both have a railway stations and services going south to Divriği and west to Kayseri. Rail travel is not to be recommended if your time is limited, but the views are superb.
By bus: Sivas's brand new *otogar* is to the south of town: there are coaches to a wide range of destinations, including Georgia.

Tokat's *ilce otogar* is on Behzat Blv opposite the castle. The *otogar* for long-distance coaches is at the north end of town. Turn right at the T-junction with Route 180.

Amasya's *otogar* is to the east of the city centre.

TOURIST OFFICES

Amasya Tourist Office: *Hitit Sk 1; T 358 218 7428.*
Sivas Tourist Office: *Hükümet Meydanı (north of Selçuk Parkı); T: 346 221 3135.*
Tokat Tourist Office is in the Taşhan (*T: 356 211 8252*).

WHERE TO STAY

There is no shortage of accommodation in **Sivas**, most of it in the centre. Here are two budget suggestions: Altay Otel on Arap Şeyh Cd (*T: 346 224 9947, www.altayhotel.com*) and 4 Eylül Oteli on Atatürk Blv (*T: 346 222 3799, www.dorteylulotel.com*).

In **Tokat** it is better to be south of the main river in the old town and avoid the new development to the north. There is nothing up the side valley. The Çağrı Otel on Gazi

Osman Paşa (*T: 212 530 6363, www.cagrihotel.com*) and the slightly more expensive Cavuşoğlu Otel, also on Gazi Osman Paşa (*T 356 212 2829, www.cavusoglutowerhotel.com*) are good choices.

Amasya has a number of small establishments in the centre at the foot of the Kale overlooking the river: small houses with character and a good location. You may need to book early to get one of them. Şehrizade Konağı on Hazeranlar Sk 11 is one of them (*T: 358 212 4499, www.sehrizadekonagi.com*). You do pay for the view. If you can sleep without the view, there is a good cheaper option in the centre of town at Safir Otel at Kocacık Çarşısı 22 (*T: 358 212 9771*). Amasya has a serious parking problem; the Maden Otel (*T: 358 218 6050*) is unappealingly on the main through road but it does have a parking of a sort at the back.

WHAT TO EAT

When you have had your fill of *misket elması*, Amasya's speciality apple, try a *pide* with a difference. The *çökelekli pide* has a filling of egg, cheese and parsley, but the pastry is yoghurt based, much crumblier and more melting than the standard bread dough of a *pide*.

In Tokat do not fail to sample the *Tokat kebap*, with aubergines, peppers and lamb meat. The *pehlili pilav*, a rice dish with chickpeas and lamb, is also very good.

In Sivas look out for *karaş*, a dessert made with berries (locally known as *karamuk*) mixed with nuts. It is very deep red in colour.

Paphlagonia

Paphlagonia is a huge spur of rock jutting out into the Black Sea, giving the coast a sinuous profile. It is a harsh environment, subject to occasional battering winds from the Caucasus and gales from Russia. The pockets of poor soil and bad communications have historically bred a race of warriors with a fearful reputation and generations of wild mules. It stands isolated in Anatolia between the Kızılırmak (the ancient *Halys*) and the Bartın Çayı (the ancient *Parthenios*) rivers, with a fluid frontier to the south in the rolling plains of the central plateau, a frontier that the Hittites tried in vain to define. The north coast is punctuated by steep mountains and gorges.

Up until quite recently the area had more or less been ignored by archaeologists, so that our knowledge of the Paphlagonians came only from Hittite sources (where they appear as marauding Kaskas, a constant worry to Hittite rulers); from the *Iliad* (*2. 851–5*), where they are allies of the Trojans; and from Xenophon' s *Anabasis,* in which they fight side by side in Cyrus' s army with the other mercenaries. They are mountain people and take no interest in the sea. Indeed, the coastal area is quite a separate entity and communications with the interior have traditionally been poor. The coastal villages were only connected to each other by road in 1975; before that they communicated with each other—and with the outside world—by boat.

Geologically the region is transversed by the Northern Anatolian Fault (*see p. 40*), which is active—as one can see from the frequent hot springs, quakes and landslides. The number of tremors in the period between 1900 and 2000 is impressive: 1,348. The best soils are in alluvial valley fills and in the decaying limestone in the north; in the fault itself, bands of sandstone provide good grazing. To the south, the igneous rocks are not good for agriculture. On the other hand, there is obsidian here in the Galatian Massif, the westernmost source in Anatolia. It has been identified in the very early levels of the prehistoric settlement of Ilıpınar, some 660km away to the west near İznik. There is also rock salt in the Çankırı area. A tributary of the Kızılırmak enters Çankırı as Tatlı Çayı ('Sweet River') and changes to Acı Çayı ('Bitter River') as it makes its way through the barren lands of the rock-salt plateau to the south of the town.

HISTORY OF PAPHLAGONIA

According to a recent survey by University College, London, the first signs of settlement in this area go back to the Chalcolithic (c. 6000 BC), steadily increasing in the Bronze Age. By 3000 BC the occupation, exploiting the obsidian and salt as well as some silver and lead deposits and flint mines, can be termed extensive. There is more to go on when the **Hittites** and the Paphlagonians meet because the Hittites leave written records. These show continuous friction along an ill-defined border. The **Kaskas**, as the Hittites call the local people, raided crops and temples (the hoard of Hittite silver vessels found in the Kastamonu area during dam-building operations in 1990 serves as evidence). They could never be thoroughly defeated and, as their fortified settlements were destroyed, they were rebuilt requiring annual campaigns. When the Hittites disappear from the world stage towards the end of the 2nd millennium BC, the Kaskas were still here, we just do not hear about them because written sources have dried up. The Achaemenid occupation of Anatolia left little trace, probably the result of low-impact governance; the smattering of roof tiles in inland locations suggests contacts with the coastal Greeks. Settlement inland remained otherwise dispersed, apart from some villages and defensive strongholds; the government was far from centralised.

But when the **Romans** conquered this part of the world in the mid-1st century BC, they needed an urban network to facilitate government and the collection of taxes. Thus *Germanicopolis* (now Çankırı), *Caesarea Hadrianopolis* (near Eskipazar) and *Pompeiopolis* (Taşköprü) were born. Finds of secular and religious inscriptions, architectural elements in marble and limestone and the statue of an emperor (Caracalla), suggest a degree of integration of the local population into the Roman way of life in the urban centres; indeed, at the time Paphlagonia was not a frontier zone and was not militarised. One of the main products on Paphlagonia's well drained slopes would have been boxwood, a material for which the Romans had a particular liking. Boxwood was used in antiquity in its own right as a very dense wood that turned well, and as a substitute for ivory in the manufacturing of inlays and trinkets. These days the harvesting of boxwood, whose growth rate is very slow, is state-regulated.

By late antiquity the cities had lost their administrative role; they were only trading places. Power had reverted to the local lords in their strongholds, with their own militias. This pattern was to last until quite recently; only Çankırı remained a city. Whether in the hands of the Byzantines, the Arabs or the Turks (c. mid-1300s), with the odd guest appearance by Crusaders, Paphlagonia retained its dispersed settlement pattern of villages and fortified hilltop refuges with dry-stone bastions and short, intermittent occupation. Commercial relations included the supply of pigs to Byzantium and of eunuchs both to Byzantium and Istanbul. Under **Ottoman rule** (mid-15th century), Paphlagonia is neglected and unruly, and the Porte is mainly busy elsewhere. Çankırı remained the main urban centre exporting candles, salt and *vefa boza*, a drink of fermented millet. Documents tell of marauding gypsies, highway robberies, kidnappings and rioting students. The population, as the Ottoman census documents show, was mainly Muslim, with a small minority of Greeks and Armenians.

Today communications and economic conditions (mainly heavily mechanised agriculture) have improved dramatically but Paphlagonia remains subject to heavy waves of emigration.

ÇANKIRI, CAESAREA HADRIANOPOLIS & POMPEIOPOLIS

Paphlagonia is an area that is best visited by driving around and enjoying the varied landscape and the beautiful, wild scenery and vistas. Few sites in the hinterland are mentioned here (the coast is described in the following chapter). **Çankırı** (*map B, 3*), the ancient *Germanicopolis*, is a modern city dominated by its ancient ruined citadel; only a clutch of pithoi, inscriptions and the odd architectural element in the garden of the Tourist Office by the Police Station testify to its past. Originally it was *Gangra*, which in the language of the place meant 'goat', perhaps a tribute to the abundance of the animal on its slopes, or a comment on the slopes themselves, which only goats can climb. It had been the seat of a petty ruler whose land was absorbed into the new Roman province. The refounded town of *Germanicopolis* sprawled on the slopes from the 1st century AD; it must lie under the present town. The citadel remained in use as a refuge and was repaired by the Byzantines and by the Turks. There were still people living in it in the mid-19th century when it was in ruins. It was abandoned after a cholera epidemic.

CAESAREA HADRIANOPOLIS

Near Eskipazar (*map A, 4*), following the route to Mengen 3km west of the city centre, the town of *Caesarea Hadrianopolis*, possibly originally an early 1st-century AD foundation, has produced enough mosaics to earn the sobriquet 'Zeugma of the Black Sea'. The animal motifs with horses, elephants, a griffon and a deer are very fetching. The town is last recorded in the 11th century. Architectural fragments and inscriptions are abundant. At the time of writing the roofless Byzantine church was being fitted with a protective cover and the mosaics will eventually be displayed. The rest of the ruins (a Roman villa, also with mosaics; tombs and a hamam) are still inaccessible to the public.

POMPEIOPOLIS

At Taşköprü (*map B, 1*), east of Kastamonou, the town of *Pompeiopolis* has been known since the early 19th century when the French consul in Sinop stumbled upon it. It was established by Pompey after he defeated Mithridates Eupator in the third Mithridatic War. The town sits on a communication route to Kastamonou (from where it is signed) and developed up until Byzantine times, when it was abandoned. Excavations in 1910 on Zimbilli Tepe uncovered columns and mosaics but much was lost in a fire. Work resumed in 2006 with a German team with a ten-year plan. It remains to be seen if *Pompeiopolis* really *was* larger than Ephesus, as has been claimed. So far, mosaics, architectural fragments, a theatre, a necropolis and a sewer system have been identified. At the time of writing, an open-air museum was planned. Until it opens, the site caretaker will open the depot for you to see some of the excavated remains. It may have been a Roman town, but from the inscriptions it appears that they spoke Greek and counted in drachmas.

SALARKÖY & KASTAMONOU

This is limestone country and therefore a good place for rock-cut tombs. Not far from Taşköprü, on the way to Boyabat, the rock-cut tomb known as Direklikaya at **Salarköy** is on the south side of the road; it is dated to the Achaemenid period. It has a number of animal reliefs and a pediment with the representation of a hero. Inside, the ceiling has a cartwheel relief that has been interpreted as a solar symbol.

Rock tombs in Paphlagonia come in a variety of styles showing continuity with the Phrygian tradition, elements of Persian and Greek influence and strong connections with Thrace and the Balkans. The museum in **Kastamonou** (*map B, 1; open Tues–Sun 8.30–5*), in the centre of town on the main thoroughfare, has a selection of Classical remains indicating that Kastamonou may indeed have a past reaching that far back—and possibly further if one takes into consideration the 7th-century BC Phrygian rock tomb, the Ev Kaya, to the south of town near the İsmail Bey Külliyesi, which shows a male figure flanked by horses. In the present-day town there are a number of Islamic buildings to admire and the castle, a Byzantine construction on earlier foundations, has been reconstructed after severe earthquake damage in 1943. But Kastamonou is much better known—at least to Turks—for an event in its immediate past. On Monday 24th August 1925, Atatürk (or, as he was then, Mustafa Kemal) drove with Fuat and Nuri, two of his oldest friends, to Kastamonou where the three of them appeared in public ceremonies wearing panama hats instead of the customary fez. It was the beginning of the **dress revolution** and the first step towards civilisation as Atatürk saw it. Back in Ankara on 2nd September, the government issued a decree regulating the attire of a civil servant, for whom the hat, not the fez, was compulsory; by November a newly-issued law stated that the hat was the 'common headgear of the Turkish people'. The immediate result was a surge in imports of hats from Italy, then an important producer. Imports of fezzes from Morocco ceased.

SAFRANBOLU

Safranbolu (*map A, 2*) markets itself as a 'museum city'—and that is exactly what it is. It has been frozen in time to its Ottoman-era appearance, and by dint of an interesting topography, it makes a very pretty sight. UNESCO's seal of approval as a World Heritage Site, together with the relative proximity of Ankara and Istanbul, have turned it into a prime tourist destination, served by very good roads. Once upon a time it was a prosperous commercial town with Greek, Muslim and a few Armenian traders all building roughly in the same style, with houses made of wooden frames filled with mud brick and rubble, and set on stone foundations.

Safranbolu stands in a sinkhole, with a stream cutting a gorge. Originally the different communities lived on separate parts of the slopes. The Turks on Çarşı and the Greeks on Kıranköy. Cobbled and winding streets and gardens have been preserved or rebuilt. Although Ottoman houses are not rare in Turkey, there are enough of them here to fill the view entirely, and one gets a sense of unity. There are no tall buildings, no concrete and plenty of greenery. The name of the town translates roughly as 'City of Saffron'. It derives from a previous industry based on the production of saffron from the *Colchicum autumnale,* the autumn crocus, and used in sweetmeats and liqueurs.

PRACTICAL TIPS

GETTING THERE

Tour companies organise trips to Safranbolu from almost anywhere. For other destinations, there are local buses—though as mentioned earlier, it is much easier to tour Paphlagonia with your own transport.

WHERE TO STAY

Kastamonou is well supplied with places to stay and can work as an excellent base for getting around. Recommended choices are the Kurşunluhan (*T: 366 214 2737, www.kursunluhan.com*), set in a renovated caravanserai in the centre of town not far from the Belediye (Town Hall), and the Taşköpü Ergün Otel (*T: 366 212 0096, www.kastamonuotel.com*), fully modern in the centre on Cumhuriyet Cd.

There much less to choose from in **Çankırı** since it is less visited and there is less to see. The Otel Sim Prestige (*T: 376 213 1200; www.otelsimprestige.com.tr*), on Atatürk Blv, is very modern and comfortable for the price.

The **Safranbolu** tourism website (*www.safranbolu.bel.tr/en*) offers a complete overview in English of what to expect. Accommodation is abundant. One can sleep in Ottoman comfort in a traditional house (Yildiz Sari Konak Hotel in Mescit Sk; no breakfast included; *T: 370 712 4535*) or opt for something fully modern (Sultan Saray Otel in Araphacı Sk; breakfast and other mod cons; *T: 370 725 2432*).

WHERE TO EAT

There are places to eat in Kastamonou, a provincial capital, and in Safranbolu, which is fully geared to tourism. In Çankırı the choice is more restricted. The Emek Lokantası, opposite the Karatekin University buildings in a basement below road level, has a good selection of local traditional Turkish fare.

The Coast from Ereğli to Sinop

From Ereğli the coast runs east, seemingly forever, a separate entity from the hinterland with which communications have historically been very poor. Until recently the sea was a much better way of getting around than the land, the latter being rugged and arduous, with extreme altitudes and rocky shores.

EREĞLİ

Ereğli (*map A, 1*) is the only good harbour before Sinop, something that the Greek colonists did not fail to appreciate: they founded a colony here, which they called *Heracleia Pontica*. Not that the place was empty before they came; recent investigations have examined an Early Bronze Age temporary cave site at Yassıkaya, where pottery and other finds suggest strong connections with Thrace and the Balkans rather than Anatolia or the Black Sea coast. In due course, with the setting up of Greek colonies along the shore, that all changed. *Heracleia Pontica* was set up around the 6th century BC, either by the Dorians or the Megarans. The name was provided by the Heracles connection (*see below*) and an alternative entrance to the Underworld was found at Cape Baba, which shelters the harbour to the north. When the colonists settled they met the Mariandyni, whom they more or less enslaved, with the excuse that they were not very clever.

Heracleia has some colourful figures in its past: the tyrant Clearchus, credited with setting up the first public library in the mid-4th century BC; a Stoic philosopher Dionysius the Renegade, who switched from Stoicism to Hedonism; and Heraclides Ponticus, a philosopher and mathematician who, according to one tradition, is portrayed busy writing in the forefront of the *School of Athens* by Raphael in the Vatican (although the more usual identification of the busy writer is Heraclitus). Heraclides was certainly a prolific writer on astronomy, music, mathematics and literary criticism, but most of his works have been lost. The claim that he was an early proponent of heliocentrism, trumping Copernicus by some 18 centuries, is apparently the result of the misinterpretation of some of his fragments.

Very little is left of the ancient city. Some of its building stone was used for the fortress of Rumeli Hisar (Istanbul) in 1452, which Mehmet II built to strangle

Byzantium. Yet more went into local architecture. The **Cehennem Mağarası**, in the pleasure garden at the north end of town, claims to be an entrance to the Underworld. Nearby are the ruins of the Roman aqueduct and of two temples converted into churches. The remains of the Byzantine castle are at the far end of Cape Baba, in a military area.

THE LURE OF THE BLACK SEA: THE ARGONAUTS

By the time the saga of the Argonauts' travels, a risky endeavour in uncharted waters, makes it into written literature (*Iliad 7. 467–71, Odyssey 12.70* and Hesiod *frag. 32–42*), it was already legendary. The names of the participants, all nobly-born heroes, some of whom have been traced in Linear B documents, was not a fixed list in antiquity. New names were added as the need to polish one's pedigree arose; some dropped off. Chronologically the trip has been placed in the period 1600–1400 BC, which makes it roughly contemporary with the Mycenaeans. The expedition corresponds to a drive to explore the lands and the sea northeast of the Aegean. Legends about the region abounded: the prosperity of Colchis was as fabled as the region was remote. It took heroes to get to grips with it. This was no longer Aegean-style island-hopping. The Black Sea was a hostile body of water, with mists, monsters, sorceresses and Amazons, dark depths and huge rivers. No wonder the sailors kept as close as possible to the south coast, never losing sight of the land. Nevertheless, the drive to explore impelled them to overreach themselves and carry on—as heroes will.

The Golden Fleece, it seems, was not exclusive to Colchis. The Hittites and other Anatolian ethnic groups had similar symbols. The Hittites hung a *Kursa*, a sacred skin, on specific kinds of trees in temples and in palaces as a symbol of royal prosperity. Its presence or absence was related to the change of seasons or the state of the king's fortunes. Much has been argued about the precise nature of this skin: a bag full of treasure and of fertility symbols, or an animal hide with precious incrustations? Whatever the answer, it is known that it took the place of honour at religious festivals and was invested with talismanic powers.

According to some, Heracles (whose place is assured in the list of Argonauts) completed his last labour, the most demanding of the twelve, on the north coast of Anatolia, around Zonguldak (*map A, 1*), east of *Heracleia*. The tall black cliffs and the gorges glistening with dark bituminous coal deposits and smelling of carbon dioxide and sulphur, make a perfect entrance to Hades, where Heracles had to go to retrieve the guard-dog Cerberus, a beast with three heads, a dragon's tail and nine serpents' heads sprouting from various parts of its body; and all this without any weapons. He was successful, got out with the beast and was released from his obligations. For the miners who work today in the depths of the huge Zonguldak mining complex (which has a terrible safety record), hell is far too close for comfort.

FİLYOS (HİSARÖNÜ)

To the east along the coast past Zonguldak is the site of **ancient *Tios***, now Filyos or Hisarönü (*map A, 2*). It sits at the mouth of the Filyos Çayı, the ancient *Billaios*, marking the border between Bithynia and Paphlagonia. Strabo (*12.3.5*) describes it as the centre of the Caucones before the Milesians established a colony here in the 7th century BC. In antiquity it was a trading and fishing port with a hinterland producing grain and wine, 20km upstream along the river. Roman *Tios* is situated on the sloping hill southwest of the Kale and east of modern Filyos. While its limits and layout are not yet well known, a number of remains have been identified: defensive walls, a theatre, submerged harbour moles, an aqueduct, gymnasium and bath, a nymphaeum and, upstream, a possible warehouse with weights and amphorae. Inscriptions in Tios, and in Olbia on the north coast, suggest transports of wine, oil and timber and possibly slaves between the two ports. As a trading site, it appears to have survived into the 10th century, when it had a bishop.

Tios is known as the birthplace of Philetairos, a eunuch (because of a childhood accident according to Strabo; *13.4.1*) who managed to carve out a niche for himself as ruler of Pergamon in 282 BC, during the squabbles following the death of Alexander the Great. He adopted Eumemes and set up the Attalid dynasty, which lasted until 133 BC, when Pergamon passed into Roman hands.

THE ANCIENT THEATRE AND THE KALE

Recent work has concentrated on the visible remains. The **theatre**, partly demolished for the construction of the Zonguldak–Ankara railway, is said to be one of the largest in Anatolia; it sits on a natural slope and is being restored. On the **Kale**, on a spur between the river delta and the harbour, a number of features, including cisterns and terraces, have been identified. Early 20th-century pictures show a few towers (now no longer standing) along the west side of the elevation. Recent excavations have found evidence of occupation dating to the late Byzantine period, when a short-lived structure was built after a long hiatus in the occupation sequence. It was a comparatively small building with extensive defences. The ceramic remains show good connections with the land across the sea but not with the hinterland. It is suggested that Tios remained Byzantine while its hinterland was in Turkish hands. The port at this time was no longer engaged in grain exports; the town probably imported its food. By 1403, when the Spanish ambassador Clavijo sailed past, the Kale had no garrison and the town was in Turkish hands.

Further east along the road, past **Bartın** and its old Ottoman houses (*map A, 2*), Amasra beckons.

AMASRA

Amasra (*map A, 2*) was in antiquity doubly blessed: by a topography that enabled it to have two harbours, and by being well-nigh inaccessible from the south. Both roads out to Bartın in the west, and to Sinop in the east, implied vertiginous climbs, of which several past travellers have left harrowing accounts. On reaching the top both travellers and horses were exhausted. The **Kuşkayası Yol Anıtı** (the 'Stone Bird Monument'), 4km south of Amasra on the old mountain road to Tios (modern Filyos), created by the Romans by carving the rock, was also set up to provide refreshments and shade to weary travellers; unfortunately the fountain is no more. The spring that fed it was diverted in 1890. What is left is the aedicula with the almost life-size relief of the governor of Bithynia and Pontus, Gaius Julius Aquila, shown clad in a toga and flanked by an imperial eagle—symbol of the Roman legions and of his own name—sitting on a tall column. Both have lost their heads. The two inscriptions, one in the aedicula and one to its left, give the *cursus honorum* of the governor and state that he had this monument set up at his own expense to the glory of the emperor and to foster peace among the nations.

At Amasra the coast breaks up into little islands, isthmi and tiny peninsulas. These over time been subsumed by a single landmass, creating a settlement with two harbours, east and west, separated by the big hump of Boztepe. To the east, Tavşan Adası is still an island, now populated mainly by rabbits. Amasra itself is a holiday resort, popular with Turks from Ankara; it is a far cry from its former status as an imperial Byzantine harbour.

HISTORY AND SIGHTS OF AMASRA

Amasra's history (though certainly not its prehistory; Tekketepe, a prehistoric mound with Bronze Age material is in the centre of town near the Post Office) starts with the Milesian foundation of a colony around the 6th century BC. It was known as *Sesamos* and was sited on the hill of Boztepe. It acquired its present name in around the 3rd century BC, from Amastris, daughter of Oxyathres, brother of the Persian ruler Darius III. Amastris founded the city but was murdered by her sons for her pains in 288 BC.

Amasra's first period of prosperity came under the Romans. The new administration chose to forget that the town had sided with Mithridates VI at the time of the Mithridatic wars, and endowed it with new amenities, such as a theatre, temples and a colonnaded street, all somewhat marred by a stream that doubled up as sewer and stank to high heaven—at least according to Pliny the Younger. He was governor of the region at the time, and in one of this letters (*10.98*) he sought Trajan's permission to have it covered over. Permission was granted and his work was so good that it lasted until the 20th century, when it was destroyed in a storm.

BYZANTINE AMASRA

Although threatened by the Arabs in the 6th–8th centuries, Amasra (halfway between Byzantium and Trabzon) remained a commercial hub and a safe haven for the Byzantine imperial fleet; it received a makeover to fit its new enhanced role. While it remained an urban centre and had a bishop, defences were strengthened, obliterating in the process the Classical grid. Boztepe was protected with a sea wall. The bridge connecting it to the mainland was strengthened with a projecting bastion known as Karanlık Kapısı ('Gate of Shadows'). The area now called **Zindan** (dungeon), immediately to the south, was walled and a citadel was built in the southeast corner. The wall on the west side was double, with a ditch incorporating a Roman bath house. The double wall was symbolic as well as practical. This part of town is not on an elevation, and is therefore vulnerable. Amasra was at the time under imperial patronage and double walls were a sign of status, as indeed they were in Byzantium. The recovery in 1993 of links and fittings of a huge chain suggests that Amasra may have had a harbour chain just like the one across the Golden Horn. The west harbour was devoted more to trade while the eastern one was strictly military. From that period a couple of churches survive, now in use as mosques. They are in the Zindan area. The **Kilise Camii** is built with small stones and brick string courses, while the **Fatih Camii**, twice as large, is a single-nave early Byzantine basilica.

GENOESE AMASRA

For a time after the waning of Byzantine power, around the 12th century, Amasra was a Genoese stronghold; it was then called *Samastro*. With the Genoese its role as a trading centre, looking north to the Crimea and east to the Caucasus, extended. Genoese power in the Black Sea was strictly commercial and was based on concessions wrested from the emperor at the Treaty of Nymphaeum in 1261 (*see below*). They refortified the town, making liberal use of Roman spolia; inscriptions with Genoese coats of arms were placed on walls and gates; a number are still *in situ* on the façade of the **İç Kale**, the citadel; others are in the **museum** on the south shore of the western harbour (*open Tues–Sun 8.30–5; charge*). By the 14th century, while the hinterland was in the hands of the Turkmen, Amasra was Byzantine and run by the Genoese. They had a garrison by 1378 and a resident consul from 1386. When Amasra came under Ottoman rule in 1460, the Christian population was deported to Istanbul and the town went into slow decline.

THE LURE OF THE BLACK SEA: THE GENOESE

With its topography, a city backed by mountains suffering from a scarcity of agricultural land, Genoa has always looked out to sea. In the 11th century its merchants and ships plied their trade in the west Mediterranean from Corsica to Spain, but things changed with the first Crusade (1095–9), in which Genoese ships provided transport. Genoa gained its first footholds in the east, in Acre and Antioch. This circumstance must have opened their eyes to the vast possibilities there: back home the aristocracy was quick to provide the necessary finance. Unfortunately the Mamluks put an end to their ventures in the Holy Land in 1249. The breakthrough came a little later, not in Palestine but north in Byzantium. The problems with running overseas trade were a lack of legal protection as well as the endless lists of harbour fees, docking fees, excise duties, gate tolls etc., which the resident ruler would exact (not to mention the donations on accessions to the throne and at coronations). Any trading nation, therefore, was looking for the magic 'privileged status' that would allow them to manage their business without interference. The Treaty of Nymphaeum provided just that. Up to then Genoa had had commercial interests in Byzantium but had been strongly opposed by Venice and Pisa; moreover, times were too troubled to trade in the Black Sea. What turned Genoa's fortunes was the demise of the Latin Empire (which had been strongly backed by Venice). The Genoese had pledged to support the bid of Michael VIII Palaiologos. When he acceded to the throne he granted them what they asked for, very possibly as a snub to the Venetians. Genoa was now entitled to her own fortified compound in Pera (Istanbul) and her own officials (answerable only to Genoa). The north end of the Bosphorus was in Genoese hands with the fortresses of Filburun and Anadolu Kavağı. Within a matters of years Genoese colonies sprouted up all along the south coast: first *Puntarrachia* (Ereğli), then *Samastro* (Amasra), *Sinopoli* (Sinop), *Simisso* (Samsun), *Vatiza* (Fatsa), *Trebisonda* (Trabzon) and in 1290, *Lovati* (Batumi). These were run by a skeleton staff including a consul, a clerk and a notary. It is their paperwork, eventually shipped to Genoa, that is our main source of information. The south coast settlement was only a small part of the Genoese set-up. Their main outposts were on the north shores at Caffa and Tana in the Crimea, locations with very strong trade potential with Central Asia. Inland occupation was more limited, though there was a Genoese consul in Sivas (which they called *Savasio*) and a couple of castles to protect lines of supply, such as Maadun Kalesi, whose ruins Caumont saw at the beginning of the last century, overlooking the Kelkit river, and Bedrama Kalesi, which controlled the east bank of the Harşit river south of Tirebolu.

The Genoese business model was strictly capitalistic and drew its main strength from the integration of local and international circuits. Capital was made to work and it was continuously reinvested. The turnaround was relentless: Genoese ships set sail even in the winter. Accounts were meticulously kept. Risk-taking was part of the game, competition fierce. The Genoese are the first to admit that they were ruthless (their main competitors were the Venetians, so there was no love lost). Anything was traded as long as there was profit in it. Apart from luxuries from the east (there was silk on the Genoa market by the end of the 13th century) and furs from the north, grain to feed the people back home was important. The Black Sea was to Genoa what Crete was to Venice, a granary. Slaves were a profitable commodity. According to Michel Balard, about ten percent of the contemporary population of Liguria were slaves: domestic slaves, concubines and agricultural labourers. Liguria has always had a demographic deficit problem, losing its people to the sea. By the end of the 13th century, Genoa was the fifth largest town in Europe; in 1293 the taxes from the sea trade postulate a taxable income of four million Genoese pounds, equivalent to ten times the receipt of the French royal treasury in the previous year.

This marvellous adventure lasted about 200 years. By the early 15th century, the Genoese were feeling the pressure from the local Greek population, from the Tartars in the Crimea, from the Venetians everywhere else, and finally from the Ottomans, who put an end to it all. The Black Sea was turned into an Ottoman lake and was closed to outsiders until the beginning of the 19th century.

THE 'BEDESTEN'

For a long time the ruins of Classical Amasra, c. 1km from the fortified port, stood for western travellers to inspect. Columns and foundations were seen lying around, the *cavea* of the theatre was identified in the area of the modern cemetery, on a slope by the old Roman road. Foundations of a temple were to be seen on Boztepe. To the south, near near the police and *jandarma* headquarters and close to a possible city gate, a building known locally as the *bedesten* has attracted much attention. A three-storey construction of 115m by 45m in brick and *opus reticulatum*, it has been variously described as an imperial palace and a market. It was also, at some point, used as a monastery. It should be seen in its present state, overgrown and immense among the chickens and the vegetable plots, before the planned restoration programme gets underway.

Amasra, in a way, benefited from neglect. After the Roman period, it shrunk in size and large tracts of the Classical town were left undisturbed. Both the Byzantine and the Genoese were concentrated in the fortified area to the north. Travellers from the time of ambassador Clavijo, who visited in 1404 at the time of his trip to Samarkand, talk of abundant ruins and empty spaces.

AMASRA TODAY

The discovery of a huge reservoir of bituminous coal in the 1830s in the Zonguldak area has brought economic development to Amasra; internal migration has been strong. Since the 1950s tourism has been allowed to develop unchecked. As a result, much of the Zindan area has lost its character, as traditional houses have been replaced by apartment blocks. The Roman town has been built over. The bridge to Boztepe has recently been rebuilt and strengthened to cope with vehicle traffic. Urban development is spreading unchecked onto Boztepe. Amasra should be avoided on summer weekends. There is only one beach and the interesting part of town is small.

THE ROAD FROM AMASRA TO SİNOP

Between Amasra and Sinop a narrow, winding road stretches for 194km, with Paphlagonia (*described in the previous chapter*) in the interior to the south. Rather than attempting to accomplish the journey in a day, one should plan a leisurely drive to appreciate the scenery, which in places is reminiscent of the Italian Riviera, with tall cliffs, blue seas and hidden coves such as the delightful **cove of Gideros** (*map*

A, 2) with its salt-water ducks. The road runs entirely in an east–west direction, so the glare of the sun can be a problem, depending which way you are going and on the time of day. Take it slowly. There is ample time to meditate on the vicissitudes of the great body of water stretching northwards to the horizon.

A LAKE, ONE SEA, TWO SEAS?

While Strabo proudly calls it 'The Sea', the Black Sea originally, well before his time, was a lake—admittedly a large one, but smaller than its present size; the northern reaches on either side of the Crimean peninsula are very shallow and would have been exposed. It was fed by the great rivers of the Russian plains and by the Danube; it may have been a freshwater lake, though recent research suggests something brackish. The period in question is that of the glacial maximum, which in human terms corresponds to the Palaeolithic, when so much water was locked up in thick glaciers. The Mediterranean was also much reduced and the Bosphorus sill an effective barrier to incoming water. With the warming of the climate and the consequent rise in water levels, the two bodies of water mingled.

Geological investigations give an approximate date for the event: around 5000 BC, in the Neolithic. The precise manner of its occurrence is another question. According to William Ryan and Walter Pitman, it was a sudden, violent and catastrophic event, fitting nicely with the Flood. Water poured in through the breached straits 'like the Niagara Falls', instantly drowning 150,000 square metres of land, setting Neolithic farmers running for their lives, while Noah sailed on to Ararat—or other putative locations. Further research though, has dismissed this theory, suggesting a more gradual development. The Black Sea today is still subject to minor fluctuations in water level (some 3cm per 100 years).

Drowned beaches, dunes and terraces have been identified on the coast: they may well conceal interesting archaeology, also bearing in mind that the abundant rainfall and consequent hillwash from the geologically young and unstable Pontic Alps, have buried under thick sediment whatever evidence there may have been of prehistoric settlements in the valleys.

The ancient Greeks were blissfully unaware of all this. They had enough to contend with from the bad press the Pontus enjoyed in antiquity: an inhospitable sea, dark and silent, with reduced buoyancy (due to its low salinity), sudden mists and unpredictable weather, not to mention the natives. In a comparatively short time (from the Argonauts c. 1500 BC to Herodotus 500 BC), they had worked out some basic facts. They knew its approximate size and shape (a geometric figure, a rhombus or an ellipse) with a double curvature on the north end, which they compared to a Scythian bow; they spoke of it as the Greek letter 'sigma', just as the Nile was a 'delta'. More importantly they saw the Pontus as two separate seas, divided by a line joining Sinop to the Crimea; each sea having reliable anti-clockwise currents. Deep down there is a reason for that. The Black Sea fills two basins, apparently formed as the result of two separate events but geologically roughly coeval. The basin floors are made up of oceanic crust and separated by a thin ridge of continental crust. Each basin is covered by some 14km of sediment. The result of all this are the currents at the surface, 2.2km up.

SİNOP

Sinop (*map B, 2*) stands at the head of a sizeable promontory (500km square) at the northernmost point of Anatolia. The promontory has two tips: to the west İnceburnu, to the east Boztepe (it means 'Grey Hill', probably a reference to the colour of the igneous rock). This narrows to an isthmus and Sinop occupies that space. It therefore has two natural harbours, the best anchorages on the whole coast. Here, Crimea is closer than Istanbul, a proximity that is enhanced by the surface currents, which supply Sinop with a speedy crossing in both directions. The hinterland stretches a long way south. Sinop therefore quite rightly feels detached, not wholly belonging to Anatolia, indeed most of the time severed from it, on a separate development course, looking out to sea, looking north.

HISTORY OF SİNOP

Sinop's archaeology has mostly been limited to the study of the visible remains; the whole promontory has only been subjected to a systematic survey since 1997. The felicitous lie of the land, providing not one but two safe harbours, attracted settlers from the early Bronze Age—as the tumulus, disturbed in the process of construction of a girls' school on the west slope of Boztepe, testifies. Fresh water was secured by the high rainfall, with the north and west winds hitting the mountains in the south, as well as from numerous springs, the result of the volcanic makeup of the peninsula, interspersed with limestone formations. Wood from the hinterland was abundant and fish an important resource. By the 1st millennium BC, a clear connection had been established with the northern shores of the Black Sea, as the excavations at Sinop Kale by Pennsylvania University have shown. The connection with Anatolia remained small.

Thus it was that when the Greeks set up their colony here around the 7th century BC, Sinop, in a way, already existed. Sinope the nymph, thought to have given the town its name, would have found her refuge from Zeus' unwelcome attentions quite crowded. Marine resources and trading possibilities were already being exploited. The two communities, both the old-established and the newcomer, do not appear to have mixed much. Greek penetration inland was minimal up to the 5th–4th centuries BC. On the other hand, the characteristic Sinop amphorae are found all over the Black Sea shores. They carried oil, olives, wine and salted fish. Another valuable export was *miltos*, also called 'Sinop red earth', an arsenic sulphate mined in Cappadocia and exported either through Sinop or west through Ephesus; it was used in dyes and to create the preparatory sketches for frescoes, known as sinopia. This was the heyday of Sinop: it established its own daughter colonies along the coast: *Amisos* (modern Samsun; *map C, 1*), *Cotyora* (possibly near modern Ordu; *map C, 1*), *Cerasus* (modern Giresun; *map C, 1–2*) and *Trapezous* (modern Trabzon; *map C, 2*). Sinop was a walled town and managed to keep the Persians at bay by paying them tribute when they struck. The story, related by Aeneas Tacticus (a contemporary Greek writer), that the town, short of men for its defence, placed women dressed in men's garb with shields and helmets on the ramparts to fool the enemy, probably refers to those times (early 4th century BC); in any case it serves as a good reminder that we are here in Amazon country.

In 183 BC Sinop fell to Pharnakes I and became the capital of the rising Pontic Kingdom. Very little remains from this period. The so-called Palace of Mithridates is a misnomer (*see below*). And though Mithridates himself (*see below*) was born, bred and buried here, his grave has yet to be located. Sinop's heyday came with the Romans, when it was the base of the *Classis Pontica* (the Black Sea fleet) and was refounded as *Colonia Julia Augusta Felix Sinope*. The original Greek town on the isthmus expanded east beyond the wall circuit. The centre of town was probably around the Temple of Serapis, now in the gardens of the Archaeological Museum. The main street ran along the present Sakaria Cd.

Sinop retained its role as an essential naval stronghold under the Byzantines and survived two Arab attacks, but eventually fell to the Turks. For a short while it was in the hands of the Grand Comneni of the Empire of Trebizond (*see p. 15*), but they were unable to retain control of the coast for long.

Sinop became an independent Turkic emirate, very loosely connected with its distant Seljuk masters. It ran a profitable piracy business and benefited from the slave trade, which at the time was booming around the Black Sea. One cannot help wondering what Eudocia Grand Comnena made of it all when she was married off to the local emir by her father, Emperor Alexios III of Trebizond, and became Despoina of Sinop in 1378. As insecurity set in, the walls were strengthened and a pattern was established with the Muslim community inside the walls and the Greeks living on Boztepe and commuting to the walled area for work.

The Ottomans turned the Black Sea into a closed lake. To begin with, Sinop did well by this new development; trade with the Crimea, Istanbul and Trabzon flourished, together with shipbuilding. Sinop remained disengaged from its thinly populated hinterland, but as Pontic trade dwindled and attacks from the north multiplied (first the Cossack raids and then the devastating Russian attack in 1853, when the Ottoman fleet was sunk), decline set in. Sinop began losing out to neighbouring Amisos/Samsun. Revival came with the tobacco industry which the new republic encouraged. By the 1930s Sinop was exporting tobacco to Egypt, France, Germany and the USA. During the Cold War Sinop carved out a new role for itself as the 'big ear of the Western alliance'. A NATO base to monitor the USSR, now decommissioned, was set up on Boztepe.

EXPLORING SİNOP

Although time has taken its toll, the original line of the **walls** which marks the Greek city can be followed. In their present state, the walls and towers are the result of ceaseless repairs, additions and renovations by the ruling powers for over 2,000 years. The walls follow the coastline north and south of the isthmus. To the west the **Kale**, used until recently as a prison (one of the oldest in Turkey, originally Seljuk) and now open to the public (*open Mon–Sun 9–7; charge*), with the Kumkapı to the north and the sea gate to the south, is still very impressive. Attacks would have come from that direction and Sinop was obviously prepared. The eastern portion of the walls, which runs roughly north–south along Atatürk Cd, to the west of the Archaeological Museum, is only preserved in patches. In their survey, Anthony Bryer and David Winfield identified over 40 bastions and towers. The south portion of the walls is currently in good shape. The northern stretch, in a more derelict part of town, has been badly battered by the elements. The breakwater may help, but large chunks of masonry have already fallen into the sea below.

The **Archaeological Museum** (Okullar Cd; *open Tues–Sun 9–5; charge*) is a very good introduction to the history of Sinop. Prominent among its exhibits are the foundations of a Hellenistic **Temple of Serapis**, excavated in the mid-1950s by Ekrem Akurgal and Ludwig Budde. The attribution comes from references to a local cult in historical sources, but the finds, which include figures of Heracles, Isis and Dionysus, are inconclusive. Exhibits in the museum chart the development of Sinop from the Bronze Age through to the Classical period and beyond. The **Gelincik hoard**, found near the south harbour 1988, with a wealth of gold coins from Venice, Byzantium, Genoa, Luxembourg and Spain, testifies to the variety of contacts of the maritime city.

The **Ethnographic Museum** (*open Tues–Sun 9–5; charge*), in a typical late 18th-century house on Mehmet Sarabil Cd, has an array of costumes and carpets.

Balatlar (*open daily 10.30–4.30*), the building which in popular lore is associated with Mithridates' palace, is some 300m outside the line of the walls at the intersection of Tarakcı Cd and Kaynak Cd (*approximately signposted*). Its presence suggests that in Roman times the town had expanded outside the walls onto the rising slopes of Boztepe. The style of the remains, with banded brick masonry, precludes a Mithridatic connection. According to the latest research, it is a Roman imperial building, possibly a gymnasium or a bath. The large cisterns nearby seem to confirm this interpretation. A suggested secondary use is as a depot, when the Ottomans, having lost Egypt, needed to import Euxine corn to Istanbul. The **Balat Kilise** inside the complex is Byzantine. When W.J. Hamilton saw it in 1836, it was still in use as a church. The simple frescoes, later reworked, suggest a 9th–11th-century date. In 2013 excavations by Istanbul University found a stone chest containing various objects—possibly relics—but whether one of them is yet another fragment of the True Cross remains unproven.

Among the Islamic monuments, the **Alaattin Camii**, built in 1214, is on a rectangular plan with five domes. Note the fine stone sarcophagi of the Candaroğullari, local Turkmen rulers. The **Pervane Medrese** opposite was built in 1262. Its marble portal is a fine example of stoneworking. The rooms once destined for students now house local arts and crafts.

BEING MITHRIDATES

The death of Mithridates VI Eupator, the last king of Pontus, in 63 BC marks both the culmination and the implosion of the dream of an independent Pontic state uniting the shores of the Black Sea under one ruler. Born c. 134 BC in Sinop, Mithridates spent his life pursuing this ambition. He probably saw himself as another Alexander, though his roots were hardly Greek. He had deep ties with Persia, beginning with his name, meaning 'gift of Mithras'; the kingdom he inherited may have included a stretch of Black Sea coast but was originally very much an inland state. As for Sinop, that foothold on the coast, it was lost to the Romans in 70 BC and later turned into a colony under the name of Colonia Julia Felix. Mithridates' relentless pursuit of his destiny—which has earned him the respect of modern-day Turks who see him as a national hero putting up a stubborn resistance to foreign (i.e. Roman) interference, as much has Atatürk did after WWI with the Greeks—is well known through the works of Appian on the Mithridatic wars and indirectly from Plutarch's lives of Pompey and Lucullus. His name also crops up in other contemporary sources, such as Pliny the Elder and Celsus. He was clearly a figure larger than life and though he eventually failed, he held for a while under his sceptre large swathes of Asia Minor, the eastern and northern coasts of the Black Sea, until he was defeated and committed suicide. He had already become a legend in is own lifetime, which goes some way to explain why he was honoured with a monument in Delos. It is thought that the Greek priest Helianax saw him as an appropriate figure to exhibit in order to improve the cosmopolitan feel of the sanctuary.

Mithridates was known not only for his military achievements: he pursued many sidelines. One does wonder how he found the time to take an interest in his six wives (the first one being his sister Laodicea, a choice expressing a very Persian concern with the purity of the line) and numerous concubines. Mithridates was a linguist and prided himself on being able to address each of his subjects in his or her own language. According to Pliny, that required a total of 22 different languages. He also had a fixation on poisons—and quite rightly so. He had witnessed his own father, Mithridates V, succumb to poison at a banquet. Poison or the fear of poison was common in antiquity. So he set about looking for a remedy, and as prevention is better than cure, he hit on the idea of taking regular sub-lethal doses to make himself immune. Celsus thought this method worth including in his publication on medicine. Moreover, in his quest for an antidote, Mithridates made his name in the field of botany (a couple of plants are named after him). Pliny himself, however, did not think much of his universal antidote made of dried walnuts, figs and rue pounded together with a pinch of salt, nor of the enhanced version with 54 different ingredients.

After a spell in the wilderness at the end of the Classical era, Mithridates re-emerged as one of the illustrious men whose fates Boccaccio wrote about in the early 14th century. At the beginning of the 17th century an unknown Italian cleric composed a tragedy about him; this found its way to the French court and eventually inspired Racine. His *Mithridate*, a tragedy of love, jealousy and treachery, was a great favourite with Louis XIV; the *Mithridates Riding to Battle with his Concubine Hypsicratea*, which Antoine Paillet painted at Versailles in 1642, is probably no coincidence. Racine's work was translated into Italian by Parini and Alessandro Scarlatti put it to music. The première was held in Venice in 1707. After that, libretti and operas on the tragic king multiplied. There were some 25 of them in existence when Mozart set about writing his own *Mithridates, King of Pontus* in 1770. It was his first *opera seria* and was an instant success. He was barely 14.

SINOP'S SEAFRONT AND BEACHES

The glory of Sinop, of course, is the sea. There are some good **beaches** (Karakum and Akliman and at Hamsilos Cove in the middle of the promontory); but watch out, the sea is cool here except on the very hottest days. The two **harbours** are a fine sight and are Sinop's *raison d'être*. The outer one is open, exposed to icy winds from the north and only suitable for small craft; the inner harbour is properly sheltered and comparatively deep; it is here that the shipyards (*tersane*) were located. Beyond that, the open sea beckons. Sinop sits on a shelf that dips gradually for about 200m or so. The water above it is not very deep and there are productive fishing grounds. Further on the level drops dramatically to 2000m, with big canyons in a dark seascape devoid of life. Here is Sinop's new treasure ground. A recent survey programme by Robert Ballard (of *Titanic* fame) has identified a number of **wrecks** deep enough to be in the anoxic water levels. This means that they have not been subject to biological attacks and the wood and other organic remains are in a very good state of preservation. Given the busy traffic with the north, this could afford a real possibility of expanding our knowledge of boat construction techniques, going right back to antiquity. The only question is how to excavate, retrieve and conserve the finds. At the moment the wrecks have been identified by remote sensing and explored with robots. A standard archaeological excavation in the deep, muddy gelatinous matrix could prove tricky. But the possibility is there.

ÇİFTLİK

Ten kilometres south of Sinop, by the shore at Çiftlik (*map B, 2*), the British Institute of Archaeology in Ankara has been investigating a Byzantine church. The structure, of which c. 40 percent has been eroded by the sea, had a short life sometime between the 5th and the 14th centuries. The location, as it turns out, was not a very good choice. The structure was twice hit by landslides; the ground is not stable and coastal erosion has been active. As a result, the church ran into trouble even before it was completed. Its floor mosaics have now been removed to Sinop Museum. The study of the remains suggests that it might have been part of a monastery built on top of a previous church, which in turn reused building material from a pagan temple. Traces of wall mosaics and of marble revetments suggest a wealthy endowment. The

Sinop Gospel, a 6th-century manuscript on purple vellum with gold uncials, which a French soldier bought from an elderly woman in 1899, may have originated from this monastery. The manuscript is now in the Bibliothèque Nationale in Paris.

PRACTICAL TIPS

GETTING THERE

By air: Sinop's airport, west of town, has regular flights to and from Istanbul.
By bus: For Amasra the main hub is Bartın, and you can easily get a *dolmuş* from there. Sinop's *otogar* is southwest of town on Route 010. The *ilce otogar* is just outside the citadel to the west.

TOURIST OFFICES

Amasra Tourist Office (*open June–Sept*) is not far from museum to the east, near the Hamam Café. The office at **Sinop** is on Gazi Cd, by the *tersane*.

WHERE TO STAY

Hotels in **Sinop** are concentrated around the south harbour. The Denizci Otel (*T: 368 260 5934, www.denizciotel.com.tr*) on Kurtuluş Cd is excellent value, with more spacious rooms at the back and the possibility of parking. The nearby Mola Otel (*T: 368 261 1814, www.sinopmolaotel.com.tr*) is another possibility (but more expensive).

In **Amasra** accommodation is also in the harbour area; it is abundant, but out of season many hotels are closed. The Can Otel (*T: 378 315 2806*) and the Sahil Otel (*T: 378 315 2211*) are both good value. The former has a large breakfast terrace with a great view.

WHERE TO EAT

In **Sinop** there are places to eat around the south harbour. Okyanus Balıkevi on Kurtuluş Cd is the place to go for some good fish; explore around that area for more fish eateries. Sinop Mantı on İskele Cd offers, as its name suggests, *mantı*, Turkish ravioli lookalikes with a yoghurt dressing.

Amasra has a staggering number of fast food outlets. A tasty alternative is the Mavi Yeşil Balık restaurant by the harbour (*T: 378 315 2727*), for fish and for the best dessert on the whole of the Black Sea: their *irmik helvası*, a warm concoction of sweet semolina, honey and plenty of nuts served with ice cream, is truly wonderful.

LOCAL SPECIALITIES

Amasra had a thriving woodworking industry up to comparatively recent times. Its fame was linked to the outstanding quality of the boxwood from the ancient *Mons Cytorus* in the hinterland, praised since antiquity. These days boxwood harvesting is state-controlled. If you find boxwood spoons (recognisable by the smoothness of the touch and the tight texture), grab them. They are excellent in the kitchen. What is on offer today has been turned on an electric lathe and is probably not locally manufactured, but it is still worth having.

The Coast from Sinop to Akçaabat

THE KIZILIRMAK DELTA

East of Sinop is the **Kızılırmak delta**, north of Bafra (*map B, 2*), one of the best preserved wetland ecosystems in Turkey, hosting well over 200 different bird species including the Dalmatian pelican. The area is protected by a number of environmental laws. Seen with different eyes it is flat, marshy and a reservoir for malaria—which is probably what the traveller W.J. Hamilton was thinking about when he crossed it in a flat-bottomed triangular punt in the 1830s. There is some archaeology around (a couple of prehistoric mounds and artefact finds) but most has been covered by the deposits from the shifting course of the river. The Kızılırmak (the ancient *Halys*) is navigable and was used in the past to access the coastal winter pastures. Much remains to be investigated. For instance, it is thought that somewhere here lie the remains of the ancient town of *Zalpa* or *Zalpuwa*, mentioned in tablets of Assyrian merchants trading at Kaneş (near Kayseri; *map B, 8*). That would have been in the early 2nd millennium BC, before the ascent of the Hittites made Zalpa the centre of a local chieftain which may, in due course, have become a Hittite outpost on the sea. At the apex of the delta is the town of **Bafra**, some 20km from the sea, which in the past had an Armenian and Greek population and an economy based on silk production and the farming of leeches (*Hirudo medicinalis*). In the mid-19th century the town found its vocation and destiny with the tobacco trade. Tobacco is still grown today.

SAMSUN

Samsun (*map C, 1*) is an old town which has little to show for its past. Excavations have been more or less non-existent and the town has expanded tremendously in the last 100 years or so. It is possibly too late, though from various strands of evidence its history can be reconstructed. In any case, Samsun is a prosperous place, and worth a stop for its mueums.

HISTORY OF SAMSUN

Three kilometres south of the centre of Samsun, at the mound of Dündartepe, now cut by the Samsun–Sivas railway line, finds dated to the Early Bronze Age (c. 3rd millennium BC) show that here people from central Anatolia mingled with the inhabitants of the coastal region. They may have worked together but apparently, from the distribution of their pottery, they kept separate living quarters: the summit of the *hüyük* for the Pontic cultures and the slopes for the Anatolians. Characteristic figurines in incised clay have a distinctive Ukrainian flavour. This suggests that the future Samsun was already playing a role in seafaring and trade around the Black Sea.

The first one hears of a settlement on the coast is with the Milesians in the 6th century BC, on the natural elevation of *Amisos*, defended to the north and east by sea, with a river and a ravine to the west. In the swampy area at the foot of the hill, there was a shallow harbour of sorts. Sporadic finds of indigenous ceramic suggest that the place was already occupied even before this. The attraction for the Milesians must also have been the fertile hinterland and its relative accessibility: the mountain passes to the south do not exceed 900m. Whatever archaeology there might once have been on Amisos, it is probably all gone by now. Looting has been endemic and military occupation probably did not help. The wall circuit is no longer visible.

Amisos benefited from the care and attention of the Mithridatic dynasty (*see p. 61*) at the time when the Kingdom of Pontus gained a window on the Black Sea (two windows, to be exact: one was here, the other was at Sinop). Amisos, previously a Greek coastal colony with an indifferent harbour, became a thriving town fully integrated with its hinterland. The Pontic kingdom may have been short-lived but its prosperity must have been real, at least for a time, as the Amisos treasure, from the tomb of a high official (*see below*), attests.

Mithridates VI Eupator founded here his *Eupatoria*, which the Byzantines later called *Aminsos*. The acropolis was abandoned and the settlement started sprawling south of it. As the land was flat, newcomers in turn settled side by side. In medieval times, Turks looking for a window on the sea set up *Samsun* and a little while later the Genoese followed with their own *Simisso*. They were here from 1285 to 1425, running a fortified trading depot. The Turks supplied the merchandise; the Genoese traded and transported it. They had a castle, a military garrison, a loggia, a church dedicated to St Francis, a hospice and a consul. Business was better here than in Trabzon, where the Comneni charged high tariffs; Simisso was also the best-defended place on the coast. Connections were strong with the outpost of Caffa on the north shore, where Genoa had successfully developed her commercial interests. Unsurprisingly, they burnt down their defences when they were forced to leave, at a time when the area had become mainly Turkish. Only a very few Greeks and a handful of Armenians remained, either in town or in the hinterland. And so it continued until the mid-1800s. Then a combination of road- and railway-building, as well as the demise of Ünye (caused by a fire), put Samsun back on the map.

A few figures will suffice. In 1865 the population was mainly Turkish and was in the region of 5,000. In 1915 this had risen to 40,000, of which about half were Christian (Greeks and Armenians). The Greeks were not Pontic Greeks, with long roots in the land, but newcomers from Ionia and Istanbul: this was not local Hellenism, in other words, but western Hellenism. The list of goods traded is long and varied, featuring coal from the Zonguldak mines, wheat, tobacco, silk, leeches, wild liquorice, and practically anything from Anatolia that would fit in the boats waiting in the harbour. Knowing all this, it is easier to understand why Atatürk chose Samsun for his historic landing on 19th May 1919 on the steamship *Bandırma*: this was a town almost in 'foreign' hands. The Turkish War of Independence, culminating in the proclamation of the Republic in 1923, was about driving 'foreigners' off the Turkish soil. With the population exchanges, over 22,500 Turks were brought in from Greece and a lot of local businessmen left. Samsun is still prospering.

WHAT TO SEE IN SAMSUN

Amisos Tepe can be reached by cable car from Batıpark on Atatürk Blv, the main road that runs parallel to the waterfront. The chief attractions on the hill are the Hellenistic tumuli, the fine view and the teahouse.

The **Amisos treasure** is exhibited in the new Archaeological and Ethnographic Museum (*open Tues–Sun 8.30–12 & 1–5; charge*), on the seafront near the *Bandırma Vapuru* reconstruction (*see below*). The hoard was uncovered in 1995 during roadworks in a Hellenistic necropolis with five graves carved in limestone, painted and stuccoed. The luxurious attire and the extravagant finds speak of a very wealthy lifestyle poised between Greece and Persia. In the grounds of the museum, look out for the **stone relief of the last Sultan, the Kaiser and the Emperor of Austria**, all in full uniform dated to the beginning of WWI. The three-quarter-lifesize relief, originally prominently embedded in the outer wall of a central, well-to-do townhouse, is unfinished, but it shows clearly where the sympathies of the local Greeks lay: with the Ottomans and the Central Powers. That was not what Atatürk had in mind in 1919, when the war had been lost and the Ottoman Empire was being carved up among the winners. Atatürk's vision is suitably commemorated in the **Gazi Museum** in Mecidiye Sk (slightly inland of the other museum, but within walking distance of it, on the other side of the busy coastal road; *open Tues–Sun 8.30–12 & 1–5; charge*) and in the **replica of the *Bandırma* steamship** in Batıpark, with life-size wax figures of Atatürk and his close friends disembarking onto the reconstructed tobacco wharf. Also in Batıpark you will find the **Amazon Köyü**, or 'Amazon Village', a tourist attraction featuring round tents with models of Amazons inside them (*for more on the Amazons, see below*).

ÇARŞAMBA OVASI & THE AMAZONS

It is difficult to forget about the Amazons while driving across the flat, alluvial **Çarşamba Ovası** (*map C, 1*). Even if you have successfully dodged the Amazon Köyü

('Amazon Village') in Samsun, the warrior ladies surface again at **Terme**, ancient *Themiscyra*, on the way to Ünye. In the past they had a very long run and have successfully entered mythology, but they proved no match for the Roman general Lucullus in the 1st century BC. The mythical warrior women are commemorated with an annual festival on 28th–30th July (a joint effort with the nearby town of Gölyazı), featuring anything from ladies-only archery to cooking.

ÜNYE

Ünye (*map C, 1*) has very little to show for its long and eventful past. The nucleus of the ancient *Oinaion*, a Greek colony, was on the headland of igneous rock that juts out into the sea and provided a sheltered anchorage. That, the comparatively easy access to Niksar and the long valley of the Kelkit, and the exploitation of the iron-bearing black sands ensured Ünye's prosperity. This is **Chalybia**, famed for its mineral resources since antiquity. Recent investigations have confirmed that it could be a suitable source of iron but expensive in terms of fuel consumption. Ambassador Clavijo witnessed the toiling and smithing on the shores when he passed by in April 1404. When the British traveller W.J. Hamilton visited in 1836, the works had moved slightly inland, where iron nodules could easily be picked up in the loose soil. The Turkish government was still thinking of exploiting the resource in 1975.

By the 12th century, Ünye had a thriving shipbuilding industry but was feeling the pressure of the Seljuks looking for an outlet to the sea. The comparatively low-lying land to the south meant that it was quite exposed. The castle on the headland, of which very little remains, dates from this period. According to some, it was the work of Andronikos Comnenos—and this was indeed Comneni land. He had earned the displeasure of the Byzantine emperor and had apparently also made several enemies during an exile that had taken him all over eastern Europe and the Levant. He and his wife Theodora ended up in Ünye, from where he successfully made a bid for the Byzantine throne. He reigned for a brief two years as Andronikos I (1183–5).

At the time of the Empire of Trebizond (*see p. 15*), Ünye and its castle hovered in and out of Trabzon's control. Diplomatic marriages with local emirs maintain a fiction that the Grand Comneni's writ extended this far, but it did not. The next one hears of the castle (then in Ottoman hands) is when the Crusaders sack and burn it in 1445. It was rebuilt: Evliya Çelebi describes a square structure. It must have been allowed to deteriorate very badly, since in 1806 the Ottoman governor of Trabzon, the powerful, extravagant and ambitious Çarşambalı Süleymanzade Hazinedaroğlu, built a truly grand palace on top of its wall stumps. He did something similar (though on a much reduced scale) in Bolaman (*see below*); the purpose may originally have been defensive. In Ünye he got completely carried away, at least judging by the only surviving evidence (a drawing of the mid-1850s by the Frenchman Jules Laurens, *unyezile.com/hazine.htm*). This was a grand Ottoman Rococo pile built entirely of wood, as is the tradition on the Black Sea, where wood is abundant. There is nothing defensive about it. It looks like a cross between a pleasure pavilion and a folly. When the town went up in flames in the terrible fire of 9th October 1839, the palace was spared. Not so the town: it burnt to the ground, including the plane tree at the foot of which Süleymanzade Hazinedaroğlu used to dispense justice. At that point Ünye lost its business to Samsun and never really recovered. The palace itself burned down in 1900 and is no more. Now the headland is occupied by green spaces and apartment blocks.

ÇALEOĞLU KALE

About 10km south of Ünye, up the valley near Kaleköy, on Route 850 to Tokat (and marked, unhelpfully, 'Ünye Kale', is the castle of Çaleoğlu Kale. It is perched on top of a volcanic rock and the steep ascent affords plenty of time to admire the rock tombs and the pear-shaped cisterns along the way. There is probably something of the Pontic Kingdom in its origin. There are sufficient tunnels, water conduits and reservoirs to back up the idea. The Byzantines and the Grand Comneni used it: there are signs of repairs from that period. The name it is known by today is that of its last owner, the Çaleoğlu family, local derebeys. The topography affords the castle perfect control of the caravan route below and of the sea in the distance. Tolls and levies must have flown in.

FATSA, BOLAMAN, MEDRESÖNÜ & ORDU

Along the coast, modern **Fatsa** (*map C, 1*) offers very little. The Genoese found it of use and had a colony here well before they were in Trabzon; it was then known as *Vatiza*. **Bolaman** (*map C, 1*) must have been a pretty place, with plenty of green and a varied coastline. The main attraction here is the Hazinedaroğlu (*see above*) family house. Old pictures show that what is there today, now jutting out on top of the stumps of the Byzantine (or Genoese?) castle, is a reconstruction. The original, also in wood, had a forest of poles supporting the precarious structure.

Further on **Yason Burnu** (*map C, 1*), or 'Jason's Cape', is a protected area, worth seeing for that reason. The wide coastal road has spared it and continues inland. Drive on along the old road to Perşembe to the minute village of **Medreseönü** to see something approaching a fishing village of old, with an active boat-building yard and people mending nets. The are no traces of Argonauts here, nor of the temple dedicated to their leader, in spite of the peninsula's name. The church is 19th-century; the pottery scatter suggests a possible classical settlement.

ORDU

Somewhere near Ordu (*map C, 1*) is the site of the ancient Greek colony of *Cotyora*, an offshoot of Sinop. It surfaces in history a couple of times. First in Xenophon (*5.5.3*), who passed by here with his men in on his way back from Babylon in 400 BC. The 45-day visit clearly proved too much for the local inhabitants (*for the story, see p. 32*). Later Arrian (mid-2nd century AD), in his *Periplus of the Euxine Sea*, described it as a small place. Ordu had its heyday in the 19th century, when Greeks and Armenians fled the hinterland and settled here. At the beginning of the 20th century the population was 20,000 and half were Greek. The **Paşaoğlu Konağı**, signposted as museum, is a 19th-century building (unusually, for the Black Sea, in stone rather than wood). According to the Ministry of Culture's official website, the stone came from Ünye, the tiles and the wood from Romania (one wonders why not from the the Black Sea forests) and the craftsmen from Istanbul. The result is disappointing, as is the **Ethnographic Museum** inside it (*open Tues–Sun 9–12 & 1–5; charge*). The imposing **Armenian church**, built on reclaimed land and facing the sea, has had a spell as a prison but is now beautifully restored. After being used as a cultural centre it is now part of the local university's administrative services.

GİRESUN

At Giresun (*map C, 1–2*) the scene is enticing: a basalt promontory dominating the sea and enclosing a natural harbour; to the east a little island. Giresun is possibly the site of the Greek colony of *Cerasus* (7th–6th century BC), an offshoot of Sinop, mentioned by Xenophon (*5.13–17*), though the logistics of his and his men's movements from Trabzon do not make a case that convinces everyone. In 183 BC it fell to the Pontic Kingdom and was renamed *Pharnakeia*. It then reverted to its original name under the Romans—and whether or not the Roman general Lucullus introduced the local cherries to Rome and the whole of Europe is disputed, but it has not deterred the local municipality from making the fruit the emblem of the town.

Up until the 15th century Giresun played a role as a western frontier for the Grand Comneni (*see p. 16*). This is as far west as they could claim control of the towns on the coast; Alexios II's victory in 1301 against the Koustoganes Turkmen was very significant in stemming the flow. The building of a fortress to the east of town followed. Nothing remains of it, though it is remembered in the name of the district where it stood: Gekikkaya mahallesi. The empire's presence was indeed effective since, in 1525, Muslims here were a tiny minority. On the other hand, the hinterland was different. The Turkmen had successfully infiltrated there and the Harşit Valley was lost to Empire of Trebizond very early indeed.

There is not much left or known of ancient *Cerasus*, though this is partly due to lack of investigation. In the harbour to the west of the promontory, old submerged moles—a hazard in the recent past—could be seen before the coastal road was built. From the harbour *Cerasus* climbed the west side of the promontory. It was defended at the top by an irregularly-shaped enclosure with a keep (presumed to be sited on the location of the Greek acropolis) and a couple of gates. Remains of walls and towers survive in the landscaped greenery of the newly laid-out park, while scanty traces survive of the earlier temple and amphitheatre. With the Ottoman conquest, the town expanded beyond its walls on both sides of the peninsula. That is when the Cossacks struck, and the castle, still an impressive structure in the 16th century, suffered. In the 18th century it became a battleground for the local derebeys and further damage ensued.

These days Giresun is a place to take time off, have a picnic in the grounds of the **Kale** to the sweet sound of landscaped waterfalls or sample the **local tuna** that Strabo praised (*12.3.19*). The **museum** (*open daily 8–5; charge*) in the Gogora Church, an 18th-century building that was used as a prison for a while, is at the bottom of the rock on the east side. The remains of the past are scarce because of the lack of systematic investigations.

The island, variously called *Ares, Aretios, Puga* and now **Giresun Island** (Girseun Adası), can be reached from Giresun by renting a boat. It is about the only island in the Black Sea apart from the odd outcrop of rock. Its Byzantine Eleousa Monastery held out against the Ottomans until 1468—or perhaps the Ottomans did not trouble themselves about it until then. Today there is little to see but plenty to fantasise about. This is Amazon country, where Jason battled fierce birds and offered sacrifices in the roofless temple open to the skies—at least according to Apollonius Rodius and his *Argonautica*. He was writing in the 3rd century BC, over a thousand years after the deed. Plenty of time for legends to grow: and by the look of it, they are still growing.

TİREBOLU

Tirebolu (*map C, 2*), originally probably three communities as the name suggests (being a corruption of the Greek *treis poleis*), is a fishing port at the mouth of the Harşit, where the coast breaks up in promontories and cliffs. It would be a much more attractive place had they not reclaimed land from the sea and built a huge car park on it, followed by a long mole. But it is still worth a visit. Two promontories are occupied by fortifications: to the west, the **Çürük Kale** is Ottoman in its present state. To the east, the **Castle of St John** is a reminder that the Genoese were active here. It houses a tea garden, so one can get inside and look around.

A third castle, also originally Genoese, stands 8km inland near the village of Örenkaya, on Route 877 to Torul. **Bedrama Kalesi** had a troubled life, ending up in the hands of the local derebey when the Europeans left and then suffering in the wars with Russia. Its present state is truly derelict and access is a challenge. But nothing can destroy the wonderful view over endless plantations of hazelnuts (*see below*). The ruins of another castle, in a commanding position at the mouth of the Harşit river, have not been investigated. The Empire of Trebizond would have had a very good reason to occupy the spot, given the very early infiltration of Turkmen nomads along the valley.

TURKISH HAZELNUTS

Visitors to Turkey cannot fail to notice that nuts are everywhere, in sweet and savoury dishes, and in snacks. Nuts are truly a staple and an important source of protein. An awful lot of them are grown on the Black Sea and have been since antiquity. The Chian amphora for which a certain Apollonius paid duty in Pelusium on the coast of Egypt in 259 BC, contained Pontic nuts, probably hazelnuts. Theophrastus, who lived about the same time, praised the hazelnut from *Heracleia Pontica*. Nuts are prominent in monastic documents and financial transactions. Clavijo, the Spanish ambassador, witnessed a ship sailing from *Platana* (Akçaabat) with a single cargo of nuts destined for Pera and Europe in 1405. In 1415 Emperor Alexios IV, in order to pacify the Genoese who had had their Leontokastron fortress burnt down by the local populace in Trabzon, agreed to rebuild it and pay reparations in hazelnuts and wine.

Today nuts are an important source of revenue for the region. Hazelnuts, walnuts and chestnuts do very well. Pistachios are too susceptible to the damp, which gives them root rot (the Turkish capital of pistachios remains Gaziantep in the southeast). Over time, hazelnut culture has become more or less a monoculture, in many places supplanting the olive and the vine that were extensively cultivated until Ottoman times. The reliance on a single crop has its dangers, but for the moment Turkish exports by far outstrip the nearest contenders (Italy and the US). On the other hand the dangers of overproduction, depressed prices and poor marketing has led some to propose restrictions on hazelnut plantations.

KUŞKÖY, EYNESİL & TONYA

Further on, south of Görele, is an interesting diversion for those who find the Turkish language a challenge. At **Kuşköy** ('Bird Village'), near Çanakcı on a secondary road, people communicate by whistling. It is said that the rugged topography and the steep mountainside are at the origin of the practice. If that were true, people would be whistling all over Pontus. But still, this is the place where they do it, and there is an annual festival in July.

At **Eynesil** (*map C, 2*) one is deep into **tea country**. The Byzantines, who possibly built the castle on the headland, would not recognise the place: tea processing is the only industry here. As for the castle, it has been reconstructed as a wall circuit enclosing a green area.

Up the valley of the Fol Dere, some 20km south of Vakfıkebir, is the village of **Tonya** (*map C, 2*), the ancient *Thoania*. It is a curious place with a terrible reputation for violence, which probably has something to do with its isolation, encouraging people to take justice into their own hands. They speak Greek here, although that now probably applies largely to the older generation. Greek is also heard in the nearby villages that bear Greek names. To the south near Fol Maden, where there was a mine, there is a church, but it is no longer used. These Greek speakers are Muslims. Documents show that there were no Christian parishes here at the beginning of the 20th century. Apostasy from the Christian religion was not an unknown phenomenon in the Pontic provinces. It was rare or almost unheard of in the Matzouka Valley south of Trabzon, since as Anthony Bryer put it, 'you think twice about apostatising when your landlord is an abbot'. Otherwise, one has to live, and especially in the 17th century, when life was hard for the Christians, apostasy could afford a pragmatic solution. Later things changed (*see below*).

STAVRIOTAI, KURUMLI AND OTHER CRYPTO-CHRISTIANS

With Sultan Abdülmecit I's act of 1856, granting freedom of religion in his empire and putting all ethnicities on the same footing, things became, if anything, more complicated in the Pontus and especially in the Matzouka Valley. Life had at times been hard for Orthodox Christians, notably in the 17th century, when the Ottomans were having difficulties abroad; the rule of law had lapsed and there had been instances of religious persecution at the hands of the local derebeys. This had prompted some Greeks in the Matzouka Valley to flee and occupy the higher marginal lands where they became socially and economically self-sufficient. Other Greeks emigrated or converted.

Then the mining boom occurred. A large part of the workforce originated from the Matzouka Valley. A benefit of being employed in the mining operations (either as a charcoal burner or as a miner) was relief from the *haraç* (the tax paid by Christians in lieu of military service). A large number of Greeks, sometimes whole villages, were thus exempt. The trouble came when the mining operations slowed down in the early 18th century. Miners moved to other mining sites and the Bishop of Chaldia, now extending his authority 'to all metal-bearing lands', followed them. Those who could not find work in the industry had to pay the *haraç* or do military service (which with the reforms was a requirement for all able-bodied men, not just Muslims). They did not want to do either.

The international pressure that eventually brought about the sultan's decision to make a steady stream of concessions played in their favour. The Russians were only too eager to position themselves as protectors of the Orthodox Church and encouraged emigration to the Russian Caucasus. The Stravriotai ('Followers of the Cross', c. 30,000 in number), on the coast from Trabzon to Batumi, and the intriguing Kurumli, are the best known refuseniks, though there were others. The Kurumli take their name from the village of Kurum, deep in the Matzouka Valley. They marched down to Trabzon in 1856, all 17,260 of them (far more than the population of the village alone), to make their voice heard. Foreign consuls ensured that their voice was heard abroad, hence the concessions.

Things, of course, were much more complex that might appear. People had to live together and compromises had to be found. It seems that in the towns religious conversion did not always go hand in hand with social conversion. People went on speaking Greek and simply worshipped in a different building. In the country, it appears that social conversion (which may have involved becoming Turkish-speaking) came before a change of religion. Some people practised the two religions with parallel ceremonies; some even had two names to fit each persona, and celebrated both Ramadan and Lent. An instance of a well-appointed dwelling built to accommodate both faiths is known.

AKÇAABAT

Back on the coast, the heap of ruins at **Akçakale** marks the site of the castle built by Emperor Alexios I in the early 14th century. It outlasted the fall of Trabzon by seven years, at which point it was stormed by Mahmut Paşa, who died in the process and was buried within it. The structure was rebuilt and enlarged by the Ottomans and was in use until the beginning of the last century. A few kilometres away is **Akçaabat** (*map C, 2*), the ancient Greek colony of *Hermonassa*. In medieval times it became known as *Platana* and was used by the Grand Comneni as an alternative harbour to Trabzon when the sea was too rough there. The survey by Bryer and Winfield reported three churches there. Today there is only one left: the Church of St Michael. It is in the middle of town, up the hill in the area between Mektep Sk and Kırlancıç Sk (from İstiklal Cd, take Yeni Cami Sk, then Sungur Sk and ask). The church was built by Emperor Manuel to commemorate a victory over the Seljuks in 1332. It is a single-nave vaulted structure in ashlar blocks with a polygonal lantern and a rounded apse. Part of it has been incorporated in the adjacent house and at the time various alterations were carried out. The mosaic floor is very damaged. The inhabitants of the house, who have been reprimanded for the bad state of the building, have taken to offering cups of tea to the rare visitor to atone for their neglect.

PRACTICAL TIPS

GETTING THERE

By air: Samsun-Çarşamba Airport is 23km east of town on Route 010. It has daily connections with Istanbul and Ankara.
By bus: Samsun's *otogar* is out of town to the west. Coaches will take you to a wide variety of destinations. *Dolmuş* services, for local transport, leave from Cumhuriyet Meydanı in the centre of town near Atatürk Parkı.
By train: For leisurely services from Samsun to Amasya and Sivas, go to the Samsun Garı on the seafront by Sahil Parkı.

TOURIST OFFICES

Samsun: Near Batıpark (*T: 362 431 1228*).
Ordu: On sea promenade near the Belediye (*only open in the summer*).

WHERE TO STAY

There is a string of hotels along the coast and they tend to be more expensive than those in the town centres. Çarşamba is not a good choice because it is near the airport, which pushes prices up. Trying inland is not recommended as it involves a tricky drive and accommodation is sparse.

There are hotels in Samsun but it is big and noisy: a better option is to choose from the hotels on the west side of the peninsula at **Giresun**. Otel Giresun (*T: 454 216 3017, www. giresunoteli.com*), by the west harbour, is one of them. The Serenti Hotel (*T: 454 212 9434, www.serenti.com.tr*) is inland in a quieter place on Arif Bey Cd.

For alternative, inexpensive accommodation try **Ordu**: Otel Modi Ordu (*T: 452 214 2329*) on Barbaros Cd, down Fatma Hatun Sk; **Fatsa**: Dolunay Otel (*T: 452 433 7200, www. dolunayotel.net*) on the seafront; and **Ünye**: Otel Güney (*T: 452 323 8406*) on Belediye Cd.

WHERE AND WHAT TO EAT

Samsun has a fair number of eateries though the town is chaotic and short of parking spaces. When you are there, try the black cabbage soup (*karalahana corbası*) and a couple of anchovy dishes: *hamsili pilav* (where the fish is wrapped around pre-cooked rice before being baked in the oven) and *hamsili ekmek* (a bap with a grilled fish inside). For more on the *hamsi*, the Black Sea anchovy, see p. 25. **Giresun** is famed for its cherries.

In smaller towns like Ünye, Fatsa and Ordu, look for something on the north side of the road by the sea. The Kerasus Bahce Balık Restoran, west of Giresun by the seaside at **Yalıköy**, has a good reputation for fish. In **Fatsa**, the Hunkar Restaurant is not far from the Post Office. For dessert, cross Route 010 and head south for the Mado Café down Hulusi Baba Cd. Mado (a name that is a combination of Maraş—the home town of Turkish ice cream—and *dondurma*, meaning ice cream in Turkish) has franchises all over Turkey and serves a large variety of sweets. It is very popular with young people.

Giresun is cut off from the sea by Route 010 and on the promontory itself there is little. The eating places are south of the harbour in town.

FESTIVALS AND EVENTS

The Uluslararası (International) Kuşköy Köyü Kuşdili Festivali (whistling festival) is held at **Kuşköy** village in the first week of July. Since Giresun and Tirebolu have no tourist office, the best way to find information is to enquire in Trabzon at the tourist office in the southeast corner of the Meydan.

The three-day International Amazon Environment and Culture Festival is held annually end of July/beginning of August in a location near **Terme**. You will need to enquire locally for details.

The Coast from Trabzon to the Georgian Border

NB: Trabzon is decribed in a separate chapter because, unlike the other settlements along the shores of the Black Sea, it has a very significant hinterland. The synergy between Trabzon, the Matzouka Valley and beyond to Gümüşhane, is what makes Trabzon special and different from the other coastal towns.

SÜRMENE & OF

At **Sürmene Kastil**, which is just before the small town of Sürmene (*map C, 2*), one should not spend much time looking for the castle. It may be one of the piles of rock on top of the tall cliffs, but there is not much to see. Concentrate instead on a much later piece of architecture. The 19th-century **Memiş Ağa Konağı** (now a museum, *opening times erratic, signposted east of Sürmene*) belonged to the Yakupoğlu, a family of derebeys who ran the area without much interference from central government. The building is a cross between a castle and a mansion, much in the style of the Hazinedaroğlu in Ünye except that here there is a lot of stone building. The inside, with the traditional *selamlık* and *haremlık*, is of interest; but look up at the painted ceilings, they are quite something.

The area is otherwise known for the first description of 'mad honey' (*Anabasis 6.8*) which caused so much trouble to Xenophon's soldiers. The culprits are native flowers (*Rhododendron ponticum* and *Azalea pontica*). Only in 1891 was the toxic compound (grayanotoxin) identified, which causes a long list of ailments from dizziness to convulsion and death.

At **Of** (*map C, 2*), ancient *Ophis*, you have reached the easternmost point where Greek has been spoken without interruption for over 2,000 years, in the town itself and in some of the villages up the valley of the Solaklı Deresi. The Greek speakers further east apparently came here more recently, more or less coinciding with the westward movement of the Laz people along the coast. Yet although people here may speak Greek (apparently the local dialect is full of archaisms, mainly medieval), they are Muslims and have been so for generations. Caught between the pressure of the Laz, who embraced Islam when the area became Ottoman, a weak central power and an even weaker Church infrastructure to protect them, they had little choice but to convert. In theory they could have acquitted themselves by paying the *haraç*, but the local derebeys had their own views on that. It was either military service (for which one had to be a Muslim before the reforms of 1856) or slave labour. For many Greeks there was little choice: either flight or apostasy.

A FALCON IN THE TEAHOUSE

Birds of prey have traditionally been very much part of the life of elite Turks, both Seljuk and Ottoman. Whether all the single and double-headed eagles on their monuments are a sign of the practice of falconry is difficult to tell, but the written sources are quite eloquent.

It seems that the migrating Turks brought the art of falconry with them from central Asia. Falcons appear in Turkish history in a variety of guises. For instance in 1357, the heir to the Ottoman throne—or at least, the one of the sultan's many sons most likely to succeed in claiming it—lost his life while out with his horse and falcon. Later evidence shows that falcons played an intriguing role in the payment of ransoms, in which context they were valued several times their weight in gold. When the son of Philip the Bald, Duke of Burgundy, was captured at the battle of Nicopolis in 1396, the sultan was able to negotiate a ransom that included twelve gyrfalcons—which he seems to have wanted very badly.

Falconry waned in Turkey with the decline of the Ottoman Empire, but did not disappear entirely: it continued to be practised in the northeastrn region near the Georgian border. Here a combination of remoteness and strong local feelings, plus the proximity of the Kolkheti Marshes next to Poti (now in Georgia), on the traditional migration route from the Caucasus to the Black Sea, have kept it alive in the Laz community. Here the birds of prey are female sparrowhawks. They are trapped in special nets as they migrate, and trained to hunt quail; then they are released. As the season is short (late August to early November), it is important to progress fast in the training. Sparrowhawks train well with intense and constant human contact: the tea house, with its hustle and bustle, is apparently excellent ground for the purpose. You may see a bird on a perch while his master has a game of *tavla* with his friends. When they go home, the birds sleep in the house.

Nowadays, however, the practice has dwindled once again. Changes in agricultural practices (a switch from rice paddies to tea plantations has contributed to a reduction in the number of quails) and the concreting of the coastline are to blame. The practice has also been restricted by central government to comply with EU rules, though an exception has been made for the sparrowhawk. A good day's hawking can result in five to ten quails (*bıldırıcın* in Turkish). The birds can be smoked or roasted in a variety of ways, including with a rice stuffing or, more adventurously, with a *marron glacé* and orange filling.

RİZE

Rize (*map C, 2;* ancient *Rhizaion,* said to derive from the name of the local stream) is where Hellenism overextends itself. The ancient Greeks dotted colonies all around the Black Sea and indeed there was one in Batumi, in modern Georgia (*map D, 1;* from *bathys,* meaning 'deep' in Greek, because of the deep harbour). There was probably one in Rize as well, although the anchorage here is shallow: it was more a case of occupying the acropolis and controlling the shore. For Justinian (6th century) Rize was of military importance and this fact prompted him to overhaul the fortifications. At the time of the Empire of Trebizond the monastery of Pharos (in Trabzon) owned extensive tracts of land here and the place was important to the Grand Comneni as a frontier post. The Venetians were also active in Rize and had their own castle overlooking the bay (no trace remains). Connections to the south are good here and Venice's main aim was probably to steal a march on Genoa. The steady infiltration of Laz people, dislodged from further up the coast by the 9th-century Arab incursions, was a movement that started with the Byzantines (who wooed them and used them to defend the frontier) and increased dramatically under the Ottomans. Their presence has obliterated whatever came before it, be it Greek or Armenian.

The ancient town was to the west of the modern Rize. The **castle** overlooks the town from a natural height at the apex of a triangle. Thick walls with towers and gates reached the shore where the harbour was. In their present state the remains are Byzantine with later alterations. The large three-storey tower on the western wall is, according to Anthony Bryer, 6th-century in date.

Today Rize is extending into the sea to the north by reclaiming land, and also to the south by expanding up the hill. It is a centre of tea- and fruit-growing, which has stemmed the flow of emigration. The warm, wet climate will make anything grow. Rize's pastrycooks are still famous too, though many have probably left for more profitable places to ply their trade.

WHAT TO SEE IN RIZE

Rize is a pleasant place to spend an afternoon once you have secured a bed. The castle affords a fine view of the sea, which can hardly be seen from lower down because of the motorway. To learn all about the Laz, visit the **Sarı Evi Museum** in the Tuzcuoğulları Konağı on Ulubatlı Sk (*open Tues–Sun 9–12 & 1–4; charge*). There is also a tea institute, the **Çay Araştırma Enstitüsü**, in Nerenciye Sk (*open Mon–Fri 7–12*), where you can find out all about tea-growing in the region. It is quite a way uphill; buses run from the Laz museum.

A NICE GLASS OF TEA

A sip of tea in the characteristic tulip-shaped glass is the great lubricant of social interaction in Turkey. While fizzy drinks have made a considerable inroad and are available everywhere in the ubiquitous chill cabinets, tea is still going strong, even in the height of summer. It will appear on any occasion: when visiting friends or meeting up at the *çayhane*, after a meal, when perusing carpets, clinching a deal, or waiting anywhere in a shop or an office for whatever reason. Boys carrying the characteristic circular trays with a three-pronged grip regularly do the rounds of the shops in the main street and of the bus stations. Tea is always on offer. No wonder Turkey has the highest per capita consumption in the world, at over 3.5 kilos.

This is a comparatively recent development. The Ottomans had coffee houses. Even though as early as 1878 the governor of Adana had published a pamphlet on the benefits of drinking tea, its publication had little effect. What made the difference was the Ottomans' loss of control in the 19th century of areas such as the Yemen, from where coffee was imported. An alternative, affordable national drink had to be found. Tea at that time had been successfully introduced in the Batumi region by the Russians. However, the Ottomans' first attempt to cultivate tea on Turkish soil was not on the Black Sea but in the Bursa region, a very green area, full of forests and natural springs. It failed. A subsequent study identifying the Rize region as suitable for tea plantations (with the right microclimate, wet and warm) fell by the wayside in the chaos that followed WWI. A new start was made in the mid-1920s, by which time it had become imperative to anchor the local peasantry to the land. They could no longer commute to Batumi to work on the plantations (the border with the Soviet Union was closed) and the newly-established Republic did not want them to leave the land and gravitate to the cities in search of work. Over the years, after many ups and downs, the move was successful. The state played an essential role providing lines of credit, guaranteed purchase at a fixed price and in creating the necessary processing and packaging infrastructure. Then came WWII, which was a blessing in disguise for the industry as no tea could be imported from abroad.

Over time, great progress has been made in standardising and improving the quality of the product. Turkey is now a tea exporter and tea-growing is an essential part of the economy of northeastern Turkey, from the coast up to the 'tea line' at 1000m. The luscious green slopes, with their characteristic ripples as the tea bushes catch the light, are as ubiquitous as the yellow and purple *çaykur* buildings (the state-run depots and processing plants), with their chimneys seemingly taller than minarets and belching black smoke. State control has gradually been relaxed and the private sector has moved in—to the dismay of some growers already worried about climate change. At present the number of people associated with the industry is over 200,000.

Turkish tea is a black tea, which means the leaves are fully oxidised. It is rather bitter on the palate as there is a lot of tannin. The brewing method, with two pots sitting on top of each other, is similar to Russia's. It is served with cubed sugar and no milk. Teabags have become very successful (they are seen as more modern and up with the times) and a successful byline are the herbal and fruit teas: apple (*elmaçay*), rosehip (*kuşburnu*), mint (*nane*), linden (*ihlamur*) and many more.

From Rize to the border the littoral is tightly squeezed between the high mountains and the sea. Settlement thins out. At any time in history from the Byzantines to the Ottomans, political control has been limited to the coast. Anyone living inland up the widely-spaced river valleys, such as the Hemşinli (*see below*), was not subject to central authority.

PAZAR, ARDEŞEN & THE FIRTINA DERE

At **Pazar** (*map D, 1*) the Kız Kulesi ('Maiden Tower') sits forlorn on a rock by the mouth of the river, surrounded by the sea and with a telephone mast inside. The three-storey structure has been dated to the 13th–14th century and a wall connecting it to the mainland has been identified. Its purpose is another of Pazar's mysteries, just like the old name of the town: *Athinai*. It has no connection with the Greek city; according to some, it is a corruption of a Georgian word meaning 'shady place'.

At **Ardeşen** (*map D, 1*), the draining of the land has created excellent conditions for tea-growing and there are tea plantations everywhere; there is not much else to see. Up the valley of the **Fırtına Dere** ('Stormy River'), however, it is another world. This was the land of the Hemşinli, ethnically Armenian but Muslim and Turkish-speaking, after a fashion. One first hears of them in 1404 through Ambassador Clavijo, who was sent by his master, Henry III of Castile, to lead an embassy to Samarkand and on the way to gather information on the peoples of the Near East. He seems to have taken his brief very seriously, though his experience was not a happy one: he thought the people were all robbers and wasted no time on the finer points of their ethnicity. Nevertheless, although he was unaware of it, he was here at an interesting time. The presence of Armenians deep in the valley is probably a hang-over from an earlier, more diffuse occupation which may have included the coast; up the valley the land is hard and rugged and all the central authorities chose to ignore it. The Armenians' change of mind and conversion can be dated to the early 15th century and it was a purely practical move. Being dissatisfied with their current overlord, they chose another one, namely the emir of İspir, who was a Muslim. They delivered their former master to the new one, who promptly jailed him in İspir Kale. Islamisation then began, though it was an incomplete conversion. Apparently as late as 1890 the people were still practising baptism 'to be on the safe side'. A thorough search conducted in May 2014 in both valleys (the Hemşin and the Fırtına) failed to produce a single Armenian, either in the villages or in the isolated settlements up the slopes, but it prompted other considerations (*see 'A World on a Slope' below*). According to the local people, the Armenians are a very distant memory. The stock answer is: 'There were some in the past, but were are all Turks here now'.

As for the castle of their original Armenian ruler, there is a choice of two up the valley. **Zil Kale** (*open daylight hours; charge*) is fully reconstructed, with atmospheric lighting at night and a tea house in the day. It is known from 15th-century Ottoman documents. Its strategic position high on a rock controlling the Fırtına Dere and the traffic along it makes it an ideal location. Much higher up, at 1800m, is **Varoş Kale** (also known locally as Kale-i bala), beyond the treeline in the summer pastures. It was connected with Zil Kale by a paved medieval road that led up to the Tatos Pass and then to İspir. The structure may be Ottoman or earlier, it has not been investigated. Neither has it been rebuilt, which is good; it cuts a much finer figure than Zil in spite of being somewhat dilapidated.

From Ardeşen the coast road continues to **Hopa**, not in itself worth lingering for, though it offers bus connections to the Georgian region (described in the first chapter).

A WORLD ON A SLOPE

The Black Sea coast is a hard sell as a tourist destination. The weather is unreliable and the area cannot compete with better-known Turkish resorts on the Aegean and the Mediterranean coasts. Still, it is worth experiencing it because of its peculiar character and its depth of history. Both elements are linked to the topography, which has played a crucial role in shaping the destiny of the region and of its inhabitants. Its impact is fast disappearing with the advent of modern engineering. The sea is no longer the main means of communication: coastal roads with four wide lanes are being built on reclaimed land; they are intended for speed of communication, with scant regard for the landscape. Inland, great feats of engineering blast their way through mountains and cross valleys on immense stilts. The terms on which the land meets the sea have been altered considerably. Gone are the tall cliffs battered by the angry waves with spaced-out harbours clutching at their anchorages. The land is now separated from the sea by a ribbon of reclaimed ground, the immediate effect of which in many places is to cut the coastal towns off from the sea altogether. Pedestrian bridges and underpasses have multiplied as the traffic shoots by, oblivious of the urban environment. These days one can hardly see the sea from the centre of a number of the coastal towns. Up the valleys, agriculture is no longer a viable option. The tiny industrious communities, the isolated homesteads that terraced and tilled the slopes with a digging fork, checked erosion and valued dearly any piece of usable land, are dying out and with them the architecture of the split-level houses, the narrow passages, little bridges, the stairs and steps that made it possible to manage a world on a slope.

To appreciate this sort of landscape and its implications, a visitor to the Black Sea should first take a trip from the sea to the top of a valley, experience going from sea level to over 1000m in the space of a few kilometres, and feel the extreme altitude compression in their ears. But which valley? The Matzouka, wide and sunny, is now more populated at the bottom than on the slopes; Trabzon's industrial development has crept up it. A wide trunk road runs through the valley floor to the pass and beyond. On the slopes the stands of hazelnuts control erosion but the tiny plots that in the past fed Trabzon with a wide variety of produce are all but gone; settlement is thin. The Matzouka is now peripheral to Trabzon: it is no longer a relation of equals, with town and hinterland complementing each other. Trabzon has gained the upper hand and the Matzouka is a mere appendix into which urban development expands. Far better than the Matzouka (worth a visit though it is for different reasons, and described on p. 27), are the Hemşin or Fırtına valleys, far in the east. Disregard the busloads of daytrippers to Ayder, where the road into the Kaçkar National Park comes to an end in the mist in a chaotic jumble of standing traffic. Ignore the tea houses and souvenir shops. Both valleys have more to offer, having retained more of their character, possibly because of their historic remoteness and the absence of large urban centres on the coast. By dint of some challenging driving—and praying not to meet the *dolmuş* on its weekly round—there is quite a lot to see on the wooded slopes, accessed by narrow, winding, steep minor roads. Admittedly one does get some surprised looks but a smile and a '*Günaydın!*' will do the trick. The wooden vernacular architecture, the granaries on stilts, the tiny rivulets, the roaring brooks with gleaming boulders, the waterfalls, the thick pillows of moss, the gravity-defying vegetable plots are all here. What is missing are young people and the working men. The past is truly another country in the Pontus and almost beyond recovery.

PRACTICAL TIPS

GETTING THERE

The nearest **airport** for the area is either Trabzon or Batumi (though note that if you opt for the latter, you will need a Georgian visa stamp: they are not difficult to get). If you visit Georgia and then need to get back into Turkey, remember to check before leaving that your Turkish tourist visa is 'multiple entry'. Otherwise you will have to buy a new one.

Rize Otogarı is to the west of town by the shore.

WHERE TO STAY AND EAT

There are quite a number of hotels in the centre of town in **Rize**: the Okutur Otel (*T: 464 214 1150*) on Menderes Blv almost opposite the Luna Park, and the Hotel Efes on Atatürk Cd (*T: 464 214 1111*) are both good value for money. If you want to eat fish you need to cross the motorway and investigate the small *lokantas* by the sea.

The **Ekodanitap Natural Life** (*T: 464 651 7787, www.kucukvebutikoteller.com/ekodanitap*) up the Fırtına Dere Valley in Çamlıhemşin (*map D, 1*) is in a different category. Here you are getting more than just a place for the night. The set-up consists of seven wooden bungalows on the green mountainside and represents the life's dream of the owner Kader-Mehmet Demirci, who one day said 'Enough!' and turned his back on Istanbul. 'Kodanitap' means something like 'peace-giving' in Armenian (the 'e' in at the beginning is to give the word an appeal for ecologically-minded tourists). It is a small place, you will need to book.

LOCAL SPECIALITIES

In Rize the thing to buy is cheese. Their *Eski Kaşar Peynir* is the most creamy and tasty in Turkey. Also look out for colourful wooden toys like small cradles that can be taken apart to fit in your luggage.

FESTIVALS AND EVENTS

Çamlıhemşin: Ayder Festival, 2nd week in June, for traditional dancing to the sound of multicolour bagpipes.

Practical Information

GETTING THERE & AROUND

The Black Sea coast is badly served for access by its topography, jammed as it is between the sea and the high, steeply rising mountains. Passes easily reach the 1500m mark in the west and are much higher in the east, in the 'Little Caucasus', with peaks standing at 4000m. Getting there and travelling around is a lot easier than it was, though, with an improved road network and a generous sprinkling of airports.

BY SEA

In the recent past the Black Sea coast was only accessible by sea: the coast road dates from the 1970s. These days, sadly, the appealing prospect of a relaxing cruise from Istanbul must be forgotten. There are no longer any regular connections by sea. The only ferry services operating on the Black Sea will take you to Russia (Novorossijsk from Samsun; Sochi from Trabzon). From Trabzon there are also maritime connections to Batumi in Georgia.

BY AIR

With the expansion of airports, a number of budget carriers have sprung up and prices can be very reasonable. Cheaper inland flights tend to leave from Istanbul's Sabiha Gökçen Airport on the Asian shore, 55km from Atatürk Airport with the city and the Bosphorus in between. Transfer from Atatürk Airport to Sabiha Gökçen can be accomplished by public transport but the coach leaves from Taksim Square in the centre of town near the Point Hotel, not from the airport itself. Some careful planning is required. (*For onward travel from the airports by coach, see below.*)

Some local airports do not have public transport connections with the towns they serve; the way in and out is by taxi. If there is any public transport available it will be a coach waiting in front of the arrivals hall. It is worth keeping an eye out for it, and have Turkish cash available.

BY COACH

If you decide to travel onward from Istanbul by coach, Istanbul's main coach station is very well connected with Atatürk Airport via the Metro. On the other hand if you arrive at Sabiha Gökçen Airport, you will find that the airport and the long-distance coaches are not integrated in any way. The only coach leaving from Sabiha Gökçen goes to Taksim. You will need to go to the main coach station on the European side and start from there. There is no easy and clear connection from Sabiha Gökçen Airport with the local coach stations. Local people will know how it works but as a newcomer with luggage it could prove trying. The new Marmaray Tunnel that connects the two sides of the strait is presently of no practical use for this purpose.

Travelling by coach, however, is a way to get to know Turkey and to experience first hand the vastness of the country. Coach stations have a multitude of operators and a basic knowledge of geography will enable you to choose the right one. Complete timetables are not displayed; departure times can only be found by talking to the different operators. The standard answer is '30 minutes'; it can be a little bit longer than that sometimes, especially if the coach is already on the road and may be delayed. As a foreigner you will get attention and service from the staff in the ticket office. If you are at the wrong booth, they will bodily take you to a colleague covering the area you want.

When you have a ticket, note that it has a '*koltuk numarası*', or seat number. That is assigned so that women do not sit next to men who are not relatives. The rule is not as strict as it used to be, but it will be implemented on long-distance travel; so do not take a different seat unless you wish to start a minor diplomatic incident. The other thing to note on the ticket is the '*peron*' number. That is the bay your coach goes from. Some coaches leave from unexpected places. It is a good idea to look as clueless as possible. The staff in the ticket office will help you to get on the right coach.

Coach stations have waiting rooms, shops and eateries to while the time away; if you do not wish to be encumbered with your luggage, ask the staff in the ticket office if you can leave it there. It is a good idea to hang around the ticket office anyway, to remind the staff of your existence. When you board, your luggage goes in the hold and you are normally given a token with a number so you can reclaim it. Serious valuables should always stay with you.

Coaches tend to be full. There is a lot of supply but also a lot of demand. Turks take long coach journeys in their stride from an early age (which may explain why the children are so quiet and well behaved).

Coaches have no toilets on board. There will be comfort stops at huge roadside cafés every three hours or so. Stops are normally in the region of 20–30mins. The driver will make an announcement containing the word '*dakika*', meaning minutes; the number preceding it tells you how long you have. Memorise which coach is yours (there will easily be a dozen or so other buses around) and make a beeline for the toilet queue, especially if you are a woman. The line is usually longer on the female side because all the children are there. The cafés have everything from self-service restaurants to shops with fresh fruit. Look out for the stalls selling frothy *ayran* (a delicious yoghurt-based emulsion) and fresh *poğaça* (savoury buns) or *börek* (baked or fried savoury pastries with cheese or meat). The coach will leave at the appointed time or thereabouts, but it will not wait. There is no head count and no one will notice your absence. Make sure you are on it.

On board some of the coaches there are free sealed cups of chilled water available, as well as the occasional cup of tea, coffee, orange or Cola and sometimes a sweet snack.

In the big cities there are two sorts of coach station. The *Otogar*, for long-distance services, and the *İlce Otogarı*, the provincial station, for local travel. The latter are often near the centre but the main otogars these days tend to be quite a way out and connections to the centre of town are often very poor. There will be taxis waiting. However, you can try your luck, head for the main road and flag down a *dolmuş* (*see below*). From a town's *otogar* you can get a bus to pretty much anywhere; if there is no scheduled service they will phone a bus en route and it will pick you up.

BY *DOLMUŞ*

The *dolmuş* is a local bus and using one is much cheaper than taking a taxi. Note that in a *dolmuş*, seating restrictions do not apply and fares are paid to the driver. Pass your cash forward (it will be handed on down the rows) and the change will be returned to you by the same route. If you are unable to work out how much the fare is with the help of the other passengers, wait until you get off. It is not a good idea to engage the driver in a conversation while on the road.

Dolmuş means 'full'; and they do prefer to travel when they are just that, so the timetable is theoretical. If they are half empty the driver may linger a while longer and then do some kerb crawling while he is crossing town to see if he can pick up extra business. It can be frustrating.

BY TAXI

Taxis are more expensive than *dolmuş* buses but they will get you directly from A to B. There are taxis available at all airports as well as at bus stations.

BY TRAIN

The development of rail transport in Turkey goes back to 1856, when the Ottoman government built the first track from İzmir to Aydın in the west of the country, a total of 130km. From then on the expansion of the network was motivated by two underlying strategic aims: moving troops quickly to the east to quell rebellions and fitting in with the grand visions of the German Empire, which attached great importance to the rail connection from Berlin to Baghdad to foster its interests in the East. Since the Black Sea region did not belong to that picture, railway transport was not developed here. Only two seaside cities have railway stations: Zonguldak (for transporting coal from the mines) and Samsun (the result of the economic boom in the late 19th century). In both cases the trains head inland, not along the coast. Sivas and Erzurum, on the edge of the Anatolian plateau, are larger hubs.

If you are planning to use the railway, you need to allow plenty of time. The official railway website shows plenty of good intentions, with high-speed trains and new lines, but these concern the west of the country and are centred around the needs of Istanbul and Ankara. Moreover, the information about trains is far from reliable. The only way to find out is to go to the station. Trains may be called 'express' but they do not always move very fast. They do not always leave on time and the arrival time is anyone's guess. One should never catch a train to meet a flight: a bus is much more reliable. Station personnel have been known stop trains at stations to allow passengers to refuel. Occasionally there are local vendors selling food in baskets on the platform, but the supply is unreliable.

On the bright side, however, trains are extremely inexpensive (more so for pensioners of any nationality). They are clean, comfortable and vastly underused: you can have two seats, three seats, a whole carriage to yourself. A brief glance at a railway map of Turkey shows you that trains never go in a straight line. It may really be, as the popular lore has it, that contractors in the early days were paid for by the kilometre, an incentive to add unnecessary twists and turns. On the other hand, trains go where other forms of transport do not and it is a great way to discover new vistas, dramatic landscapes, secret valleys and rivers meandering in the wilderness.

The Istanbul station on the Asian shore (Haydarpaşa Garı) from which the trains east should depart, was closed for refurbishment at the time of writing. Trains now go from Pendik. To get there from Sabiha Gökcen Airport you should in theory take bus IETT E-9 from just outside Arrivals to Pendik-IDO (tickets from the nearby kiosk) but if it proves elusive (as it has of late), Pendik is a short taxi ride away. At Pendik note that the station is underground but the ticket office is at street level, round the corner to the left.

BY CAR

To be completely independent and to see all you want to in the time you have at your disposal, travelling by car makes the most sense. Not that it is recommended to drive all the way from Istanbul or Ankara to the Black Sea: but once you are there you can hire a car locally to reach a number of sites that are not on main bus routes.

All the towns have a number of operators to choose from. Some of the businesses may have familiar Western names, but that is where the similarity ends. Make sure when you pick up your car to check the basics such as the presence of a spare wheel in the boot and a jack (every piece of it); check the windscreen for cracks, note the various bumps and so on; take a few pictures.

Travelling with your own transport affords great freedom and pleasure but it does come at a price. The road network is of variable quality (though it has been recently much improved). Unfortunately (or fortunately) that improvement is still an ongoing business. Roadworks are everywhere, though most of the time there does not seem to be much work actually going on. It is a very slow process that entails piles of chippings, gravel, unfinished surfaces, no road markings etc. Driving slowly is the only answer, with the adjunct of never driving at night.

Petrol is available near and in towns. The countryside is pretty empty and there is nothing in the villages.

MAPS

On the whole, the choice of maps on the market for the Pontic provinces of Turkey is very limited, though it is an improvement on the situation some years back. Unlike the western shores of Turkey, this area is still waiting for its own map and as long as everything has to fit on a single sheet from Istanbul to Van, practical considerations will mean that the best scale one can hope for is 1:800,000 which is to say, 1cm for every 8km. By comparison a standard European road atlas is four times as detailed.

On the whole, destinations are well signposted along the main traffic axes. Beyond that, on the smaller roads, there is plenty of scope for adventure. It is best to explore with plenty of time ahead and a full tank.

ACCOMMODATION

As elsewhere in Turkey, accommodation has multiplied in the Pontic region, but that does not mean that there was no infrastructure before this. Cities and small towns have always had some accommodation available and it is worth investigating the hotels where Turks would go. They tend to be cheaper—but also more basic; for instance, they may not offer internet access, which is now standard in accommodation intended for foreign tourists. It all depends on how basic you are prepared to go.

Do ask to see the room before you confirm. Have a good look, feel the bed, enquire after the availability of hot water and test it yourself. If you are told you have to let it run for 20mins, it is a bad sign. Either look for somewhere else or settle for a cold shower. Washing facilities are rarely *en suite*. If you want a non-smoking room you may be offered a space 'purified' by air freshener, perhaps worse than the original cigarette aroma.

Breakfast is normally not on offer but that should not be a deterrent. Breakfast in eastern Turkish hotels is rarely lucullan in any case. The bread is uninteresting, the fruit juice probably won't be fresh, and the cheese and vegetables will have nothing of the farmhouse appeal you might be hoping for. There may not be coffee either (though if you're travelling with a jar of instant granules, hot water is always available). Milk is not widely on offer. You can try and ask for '*süt*', but it is not taken in Turkish coffee or tea and is difficult to come by.

In any case it is much better to forgo breakfast at the hotel and head for a *kahvaltı salonu* (a breakfast salon). Here you can compose your breakfast at leisure, indulge in honey and *kaymak* (a sort of clotted cream), try *pekmez* (a grape juice concentrate traditionally used as sugar substitute with yoghurt), have freshly-cut vegetables, order an egg, insist on bread straight from the bakery, and even try your luck and ask for a Turkish coffee. It is well worth the extra expense. Alternatively, if you spot a *pastane* with seating for customers, you could go there: there will be tea (and hot water for your instant coffee) as well as *böreks* or a selection of biscuits and pastries baked on the premises.

EATING

The Black Sea region of Turkey is little visited by tourists and the offering in terms of places to eat is very different from Istanbul or the Aegean resorts. At the end of each chapter of this guide some general tips are given, and an indication of which towns are better supplied with places to eat. Often it is not possible to do more than that. Large cities like Trabzon, or tourist destinations such as Safranblolu, do have restaurants, but even so it is not easy to pinpoint particular establishments as more recommendable than others. Anyone can open a restaurant in Turkey and though hygiene norms are very strict on paper, the fact is that if your system is not acclimatised, you might get an upset stomach. If you are at all unsure, insist on sealed water and only eat cooked dishes, nothing raw (including vegetables).

Do not expect a printed menu posted outside the restaurant. You will find out what is on offer after you have been seated—and the choice may be limited. The food served will be what they have available at the time: it will depend on the day and on the time of day. On the other hand, as a foreigner, you will have novelty value and will receive extra attention. If you have a couple of words of Turkish, this is the time to use them!

A small number of restaurants now have websites. These are usually the more expensive ones. The food in the nearby *lokanta* will often be just the same, and half the price.

CLIMATE & WHEN TO GO

While the official Turkish tourism portal plays down the attractions of the Black Sea coast as a beach holiday destination because, as they put it, 'the cloud is more common than the sun', there is no doubt that the area is gearing itself to a different kind of visitor, someone who is ready to appreciate the luscious greenness, the history, the high peaks and the variety of landscapes. All this comes at a price: temperatures are not very high and the climate is wet. Summers on the coast are warm and humid but the sea is cool at the best of times. May–June are good months to plan a visit. There will be less rain than in the summer and temperatures will be picking up. However, in June the average temperatures will be c. 4–5 degrees centigrade cooler than the Aegean or Mediterranean coasts. It will be possible to swim some days. The main problem with the climate is that it is unpredictable at any time of year and settled spells of fine weather are rare.

PRONUNCIATION GUIDE

Turkish was originally written in the Arabic script. In 1928 Atatürk introduced a modified Latin alphabet of 29 letters, the modification designed to take into account the specific requirements of the Turkish language.

Turkish is phonetic, unlike English; so it is easy to read and pronounce it—especially useful if you need to ask for directions. All letters are sounded; there are no dipththongs. The letters are pronounced as follows:

A	a	as in adamant
E	e	as in elephant
İ	i	as in Italy
I	ı	the 'schwa' sound, like the 'a' in Cola
J	j	used in loan words (*'projesi'*) and pronounced like Jacques
O	o	as in pond
Ö	ö	as in blur
U	u	as in luminous
Ü	ü	as in Zürich
Ç	ç	a soft 'ch', as in charming
C	c	a soft G, as in Geneva
G	g	a hard G, as in Gap
Ğ	ğ	a consonant that is not voiced. If it is between two vowels, it separates them and will lengthen the first one. At the end of a word (dağ) it is not pronounced.
Ş	ş	like the 'sh' in dish
Y	y	as in yeti

Glossary

Aedicula A small, free-standing construction with an opening framed by columns, or its representation on a flat surface, in which case it acts as an ornamental frame, e.g. to house a statue or a portrait.

Ashlar A construction style that uses squared stone blocks.

Ak Koyunlu ('White-Tailed Sheep') A Turkic tribal federation, mainly Sunni Muslims, that ruled parts of Eastern Turkey, Armenia, Azerbaijan northern Iraq and Iran from 1378 to 1508.

Alevi A religious minority combining Anatolian folk traditions and elements of Sufism, a mystic branch of Islam. Alevis are also known as Kızıl Baş from the red caps worn by the followers of Shah Ismail, who was defeated by the Ottomans at Çaldıran in 1514.

Anahita A goddess of fertility and wisdom of Persian origin.

Archimetallurgoi A term referring to the Greeks who ran mining operations in the Pontus.

Belediye A town hall

Bulla The seal in lead (or, rarely, gold) applied to an important document; by extension the document itself, a bull.

Bedesten A covered market. The word derives from '*bez*' meaning cloth, an important and valuable asset.

Chalcolithic The very beginning of the Bronze Age, when native copper is worked unalloyed.

Cavea The semicircular seating arrangement of a Classical theatre, frequently built against the natural slope of a hill.

Çayhane A place to drink tea and soft drinks and to play cards and backgammon.

Cemevi The building in which Alevi (*qv*) worship takes place.

Cross in square A typical middle-to-late Byzantine church plan. The interior space is divided into three aisles (the middle one normally wider) with apses at the east end. The space is further subdivided with the insertion of a dome supported by four pillars roughly halfway along the central aisle, thereby creating a cruciform pattern.

Derebeys Local warlords exercising authority with or without the consent of the central authority.

Despoina A Byzantine courtesy title for upper-class women.

Emporium A large trading location.

Faïence A type of glazed ceramic with a characteristic blue colour.

Floruit The most prosperous time in the life of a settlement, of a region or of an individual.

Garum A fish-based sauce widely used in antiquity and said to have tasted like the Vietnamese Nuoc Mam.

Hac (Haj) The holy pilgrimage to

Mecca, a duty for all pious Muslims.

Haraç A tax paid by non Muslims in the Ottoman Empire in lieu of military service.

Haremlık The secluded part of a traditional Turkish house, with no direct outside access, for women only.

Hatun In the Ottoman world, a female honorific title.

Heliocentrism The astronomical model whereby the sun is stationary and the planets revolve around it.

Hexastyle A temple with six columns fronting its porch.

Hierodule A compound Greek word designating a person working for the religious authorities either as prostitutes or as manual workers.

Hillwash Debris accumulated though the action of gravity at the foot of a cliff or a slope.

Hodegetria Literally 'She who shows the way'. It refers to an icon type in which the Virgin hold the infant Jesus and points to him as the route to salvation.

Hüyük A man made elevation, the result of a long sequence of occupation. Also called a tell or a mound.

Iwan Opening closed on three sides in a colonnaded courtyard of a large Islamic public building.

Kara Koyunlu ('Black-Tailed Sheep') A Turkic tribal federation, mainly Shiite Muslims, that ruled parts of Armenia, Azerbaijan, northwestern Iran, eastern Turkey and Iraq from about 1375 to 1468. Compare Ak Koyunlu, above.

Kufic A decorative form of Arabic script developed in the 7th century.

Külliye A building complex around a mosque and managed as a single institution. It can contain a caravanserai, a mausoleum, a school and a hospital.

Kümbet A mausoleum, originally developed in pre-Islamic Iran, characterised by a polygonal or round body with two chambers topped by a tall conical roof.

Linear B A form of script used by the Mycenaeans in the mid-2nd millennium BC.

Manicheism A system of religious doctrines originally developed in Iran in the 3rd century AD and based on the primordial conflict between good and evil and light and darkness.

Mihrab The niche in the interior wall of a mosque indicating the direction of Mecca.

Minber (also Mimber) Pulpit in a mosque from where sermons are delivered.

Mamluks A military caste with a time span from the 9th–19th centuries and assembling warriors of various ethnicities; its heyday was in medieval Egypt.

Medrese An Islamic educational institution, normally but not always attached to a mosque.

Nakharar An honorific title in medieval Armenia.

Narthex The entrance area of an early Christian and Byzantine church located west of the nave.

Nymphaeum In the Classical world, a natural feature or a monument sacred to the nymphs and associated with water.

Oculus In Latin, 'eye'. The opening in a dome allowing light (and the rain) in.

Opus reticulatum A type of facing on Roman concrete or mortared rubble walls, made of diamond-shaped elements set on a point and looking like a net, hence the name.

Opus sectile A wall and floor covering made of thin pieces of different stone cut to shape.

Opus alexandrinum A form of mosaic in which decorative elements are inlaid in the stone floor forming intricate geometric patterns; first used in Byzantium in the 9th century and afterwards in medieval Europe.

Paşa A high-ranking title in the Ottoman administration and army.

Pastophoria The dressing rooms on either side of the apse in an Orthodox church.

Pekmez A sweetener made of concentrated grape juice. Much used in the past in Turkey when honey was expensive and sugar was not available.

Pithos (pl. pithoi) Ancient storage jar of very large dimensions.

Proconnesian marble A coarse marble from the island of *Proconnesus* in the Sea of Marmara (now Marmara adası), normally in various shades of grey.

Saltukid A local Turkmen dynasty in Erzurum that came to power after the Battle of Manzikert (1071), in which they assisted the conquering Seljuk army.

Selamlık The part of a traditional Turkish house reserved for men, with direct outside access.

Şerefe The wooden balcony surrounding the upper part of a minaret.

Spolia The reuse from late antiquity onwards of masonry elements of Classical monuments, as building material or ornament.

Stavropegic A religious institution in the East which is self-governing and self-determining as it is not subject to the local bishop; it refers directly to the Patriarch.

Tetrastyle A temple with four columns in the front.

Türbe A Muslim tomb, often taking the form of a mausoleum in the grounds of a mosque.

Tekke Monastic complex in the Muslim world.

Uncial A kind of script formed of entirely of capital letters with rounded shapes, used in Greek and Latin manuscripts from the 4th–8th centuries.

Urartian A designation by the Assyrians of the people (and of their language) living in the Lake Van region from the 13th–6th centuries BC.

Valide Sultan An honorific Ottoman title designating the mother of the ruling sultan.

Venationes Games that involved the hunting of wild beasts in an amphitheatre, a Roman practice.

Yayla/kışla Terms indicating summer and winter pastures in Turkish.

Timeline

400,000 BC Palaeolithic occupation is attested in the western part of the Black Sea. The geography is very different.

12000 BC End of glaciations. Ice sheets retreat. It is warming up. Steppe turns to forest. The geography is again very different.

6000 BC Chalcolithic occupation attested in Paphlagonia.

5000 BC An approximate time for the breaching of the Bosphorus; the lake becomes a sea.

3000 BC Exploitation of obsidian and rock salt in Paphlagonia.

1450 BC The Kaskas, people from the mountains of Pontic Anatolia whose relations with the Hittites are strained, make their first appearance in a Hittite written document.

1600–1400 BC The time of the Argonauts and their adventures.

7th century BC Beginning of Greek coastal colonisation.

400 BC Xenophon and his men sight the Pontus from the heights south of Trabzon.

281 BC Mithridates Ktistes declares himself king. Beginning of the Kingdom of Pontus.

280–180 BC Amasya (then *Amaseia*) is the capital of the Kingdom of Pontus.

180 BC King Pharnakes moves the capital to Sinop.

92 BC The Romans set up the Euphrates as their eastern frontier and fortify it. The picture is much the same when Byzantium succeeds Rome, and the Parthians are followed by the Sassanids. This is a border area and remains unstable to the east and south.

63 BC End of Pontic Kingdom. The province becomes first Roman, then Byzantine.

AD **632–850** Muslim Arabs make incursions and destabilize the region. With the loss of Tbilisi, the Georgian power centre moves south and west into the Hopa hinterland.

9th century The Laz are destabilised by the Arabs and start moving west along the coast from Georgia.

1071 Battle of Manzikert. The Seljuk Turks from the east defeat the Byzantines. A new player enters the scene. They are here to stay.

1204 The Empire of Trebizond comes into existence.

1214 Sinop falls to the Seljuks. Gradually control of the western portion of the coast is lost to the Seljuks and other Turkmen. By the mid-14th century the Cepni Turkmen control the Harşit Valley down to the sea.

1250–1456 The Black Sea is opened to foreign traders.

1256–1335 The Mongol Il Khanate rules large tracts of Anatolia. They exact tribute and provide peace. Trade with the east via Tabriz blooms.

1403–4 The Spanish ambassador Ruy González de Clavijo travels from Byzantium to the court of Timur in Samarkand and leaves abundant notes.

1461 End of the Trebizond Empire. The Black Sea becomes an Ottoman lake and remains so until the end of the 18th century.

Mid-19th century Trabzon booms once again, thanks to the building of a carriage road to Tabriz. The days of the camel caravans are over. The same period also sees the heyday of Samsun.

1828–1921 A number of wars with Russia on the Turco-Caucasian border. Kars and Erzurum fall in and out of Russian control.

1919 Atatürk lands in Samsun

July 1923 Treaty of Lausanne. Turkey attains her present borders.

Index

MAP D
Black Sea
GEORGIA
ARMENIA
AZERBAIJAN
IRAQ
SYRIA
Samtredia
Gori
Tbilisi
Ozurgeti
Batumi
Ahalcihe
Hopa
Borçka
Şavşat
Fındıklı
CANKURTARAN GEÇIDI
Hamamlı
Ardanuç
Pazar
Ardeşen
Artvin
Yeni Rabat
Çamlihemşin
Çayeli
Lake Çildir
Gyowmri
Vanajor
Yusufeli
Işhan Kilise
Dört Kilise
Oltu Çayı
Kars
Ani
Tortum Gölü
Vank Monastery
Uzungöl
Ispir
Çoruh Nehri
Bağbaşı
Uzundere
Yerevan
Sarıkamış
Tuzluca
2918m
Kop Dağı
Horasan
Iğdir
Ağrı Dağı (Ararat)
5137m
Balik Gölü
Pasinler
Köprüköy
Aşkale
Ilıca
Erzurum
Ağrı
IPEK GEÇIDI
Doğubayazit
Ishak Paşa Sarayı
Aras Nehri
Ilıca
Patnos
Erçis
Çaldıran
Varto
Kale Kayalıdere
Malazgirt
Muradiye
BUĞLARI GEÇIDI
4058m
Süphan Dağı
Erçek Gölü
Ahlat
Adilcevaz
Ayanis
Bingöl
Muş
Nemrut Dağı
2935m
Van Gölü
Özalp
Arak Vank
Van
Toprakkale
Yedi Kilise
Reşadiye
Van Kalesi
Hoşap Kale
Tatvan
Akhtamar Adası
Hoşap Suyu
GÜZELDERE GEÇIDI
Lice
Tilki Tepe
Zernek Barajı
Çavuştepe
Albayrak
Bitlis
Göründü
Gevaş
Hizan (Karasu)
Malabadi Köprüsü
Başkale
Silvan
Yanarsu
HAKKARI DAĞLARI
Siirt
Batman
Dicle Nehri (Tigris)
Hasankeyf
Şırnak
Hakkari
Yüksekova
Gercüş
El Hadra
Dargecit
3607m
Sümbül Dağı
Mor Yakub
2114m
Cudi Dağı
Midyat
Cizre
Mor Gabriel
Mardin
Deir al Zafaran
Dara
Mor Augen
Kızıltepe
Nusaybin
Al Ḥasakah
N
0 50 miles
0 50 kms

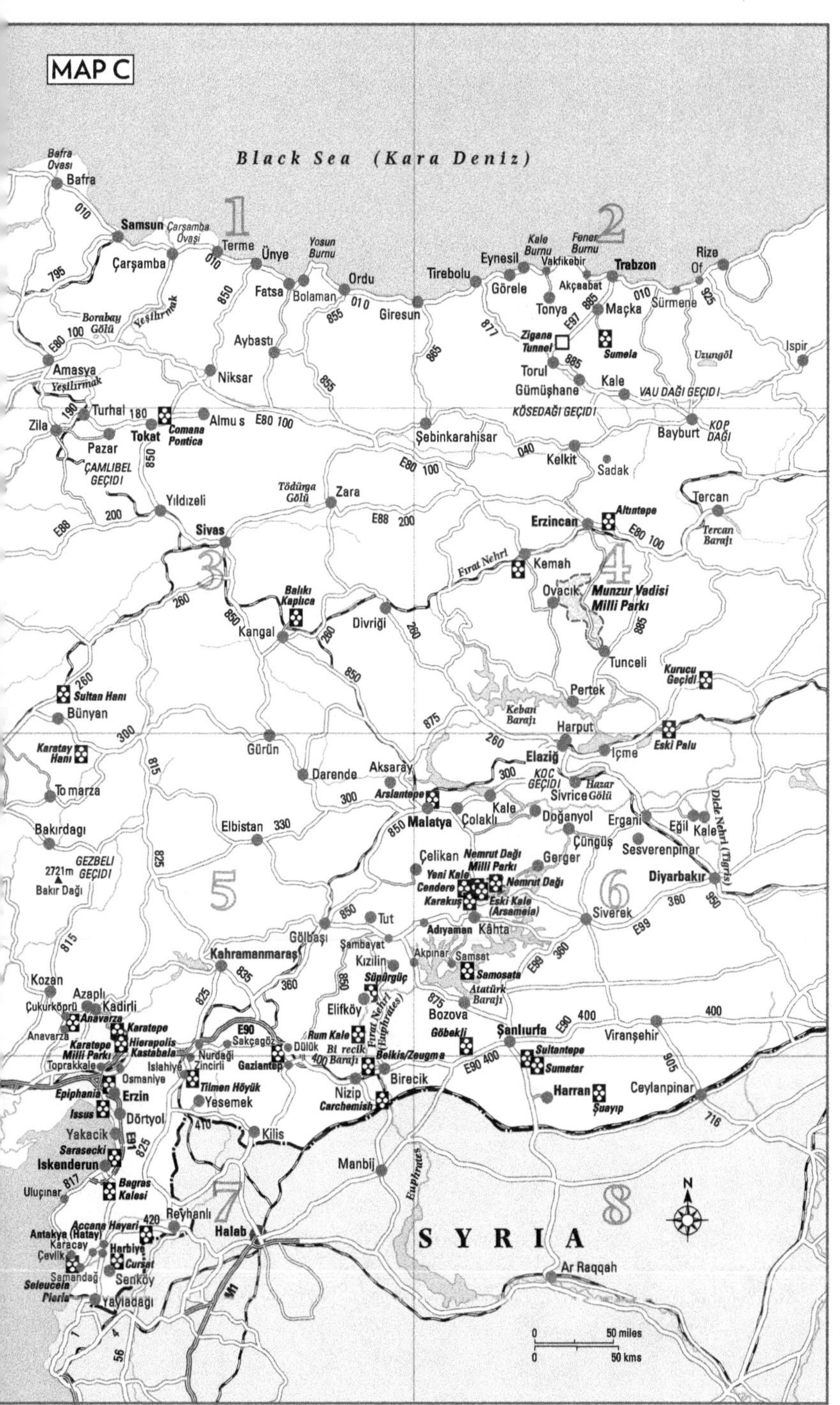
MAP C
Black Sea (Kara Deniz)
Bafra
Samsun
Çarşamba
Terme
Ünye
Fatsa
Bolaman
Ordu
Giresun
Tirebolu
Görele
Eynesil
Vakfıkebir
Akçaabat
Trabzon
Of
Rize
Sürmene
Maçka
Tonya
Zigana Tunnel
Sumela
Uzungöl
Ispir
Torul
Gümüşhane
Kale
Amasya
Niksar
Aybastı
Turhal
Tokat
Comana Pontica
Almus
Zila
Pazar
Şebinkarahisar
Kelkit
Sadak
Bayburt
KOP DAĞI
Yıldızeli
Zara
Sivas
Erzincan
Altıntepe
Tercan
Kemah
Ovacık
Munzur Vadisi Milli Parkı
Balıkı Kaplıca
Kangal
Divriği
Tunceli
Kurucu Geçidi
Sultan Hanı
Bünyan
Pertek
Keban Barajı
Harput
Elazığ
İçme
Eski Palu
Karatay Hanı
Gürün
Darende
Aksaray
Arslantepe
Malatya
Çolaklı
Kale
Doğanyol
Sivrice
Hazar Gölü
Ergani
Eğil
Kale
Tomarza
Bakırdağı
Elbistan
Çelikan
Nemrut Dağı Milli Parkı
Gerger
Çüngüş
Sesverenpinar
Diyarbakır
Bakır Dağı
Yeni Kale
Cendere
Karakuş
Nemrut Dağı
Eski Kale (Arsameia)
Siverek
Tut
Adıyaman
Kâhta
Gölbaşı
Kahramanmaraş
Şambayat
Akpınar
Samsat
Samosata
Atatürk Barajı
Kızılin
Süpürgüç
Elifköy
Bozova
Kozan
Azaplı
Kadirli
Anavarza
Karatepe
Hierapolis
Kastabala
Karatepe Milli Parkı
Toprakkale
Sakçagöz
Nurdağı
Zincirli
Islahiye
Dülük
Rum Kale
Birecik Barajı
Gaziantep
Belkis/Zeugma
Göbekli
Şanlıurfa
Sultantepe
Sumatar
Viranşehir
Osmaniye
Epiphania
Erzin
Issus
Tilmen Höyük
Yesemek
Nizip
Carchemish
Birecik
Harran
Şuayıp
Ceylanpinar
Dörtyol
Yakacik
Sarasecki
Iskenderun
Kilis
Manbij
Euphrates
Uluçınar
Bagras Kalesi
Reyhanlı
Halab
SYRIA
Antakya (Hatay)
Accana Hayari
Karacay
Çevlik
Harbiye
Cursat
Samandağ
Seleucela Pieria
Senköy
Yayladağı
Ar Raqqah
N
50 miles
50 kms

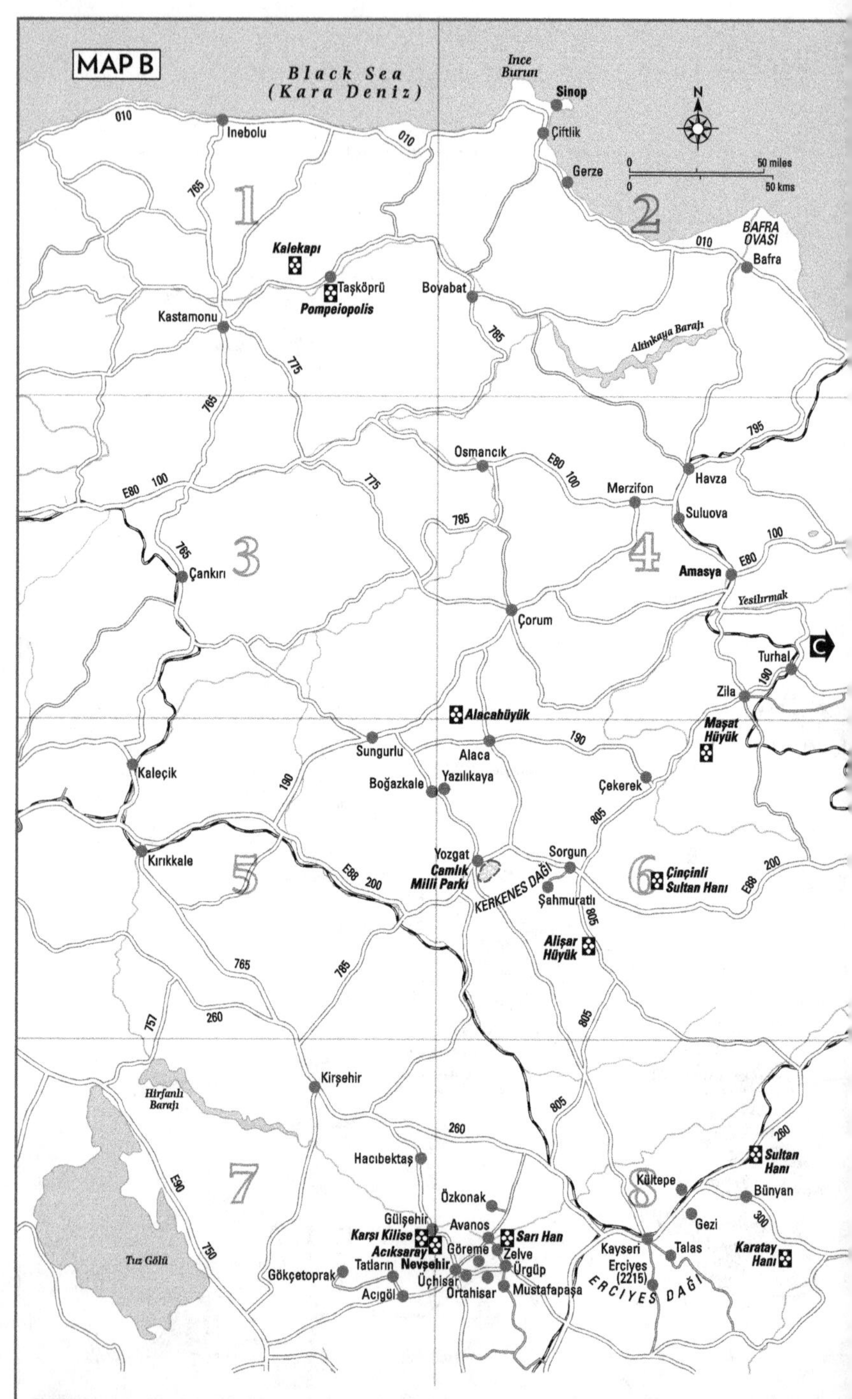
MAP B
Black Sea
(Kara Deniz)
Ince Burun
Sinop
Çiftlik
Gerze
Inebolu
Kalekapı
Taşköprü
Pompeiopolis
Boyabat
Kastamonu
BAFRA OVASI
Bafra
Altınkaya Barajı
Osmancık
Havza
Merzifon
Suluova
Amasya
Yesilırmak
Çankırı
Çorum
Turhal
Zila
Maşat Hüyük
Alacahüyük
Sungurlu
Alaca
Boğazkale
Yazılıkaya
Çekerek
Kaleçik
Kırıkkale
Yozgat
Çamlık Milli Parkı
Sorgun
KERKENES DAĞI
Şahmuratlı
Çinçinli Sultan Hanı
Alişar Hüyük
Kirşehir
Hirfanlı Barajı
Hacıbektaş
Sultan Hanı
Kültepe
Bünyan
Özkonak
Gülşehir
Avanos
Gezi
Karşı Kilise
Sarı Han
Acıksaray
Göreme
Zelve
Kayseri
Talas
Karatay Hanı
Tuz Gölü
Gökçetoprak
Tatların
Nevşehir
Ürgüp
Erciyes (2215)
Üçhisar
Ortahisar
Mustafapaşa
ERCIYES DAĞI
Acıgöl
50 miles
50 kms

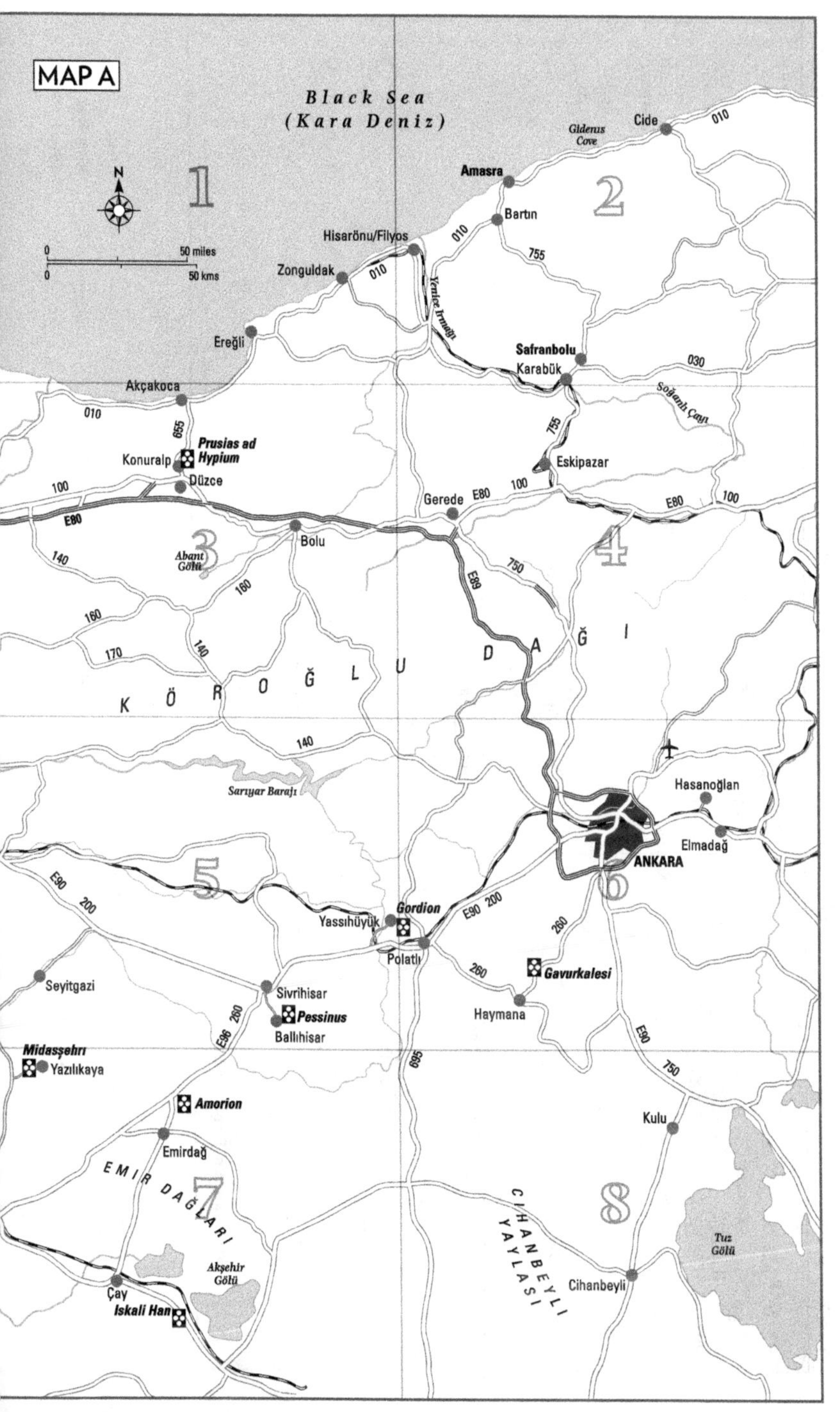

MAP A
Black Sea
(Kara Deniz)
N
0
50 miles
0
50 kms
1
2
3
4
5
6
7
8
Gideros Cove
Cide
Amasra
Bartın
Hisarönü/Filyos
Zonguldak
Ereğli
Akçakoca
Yenice Irmağı
Safranbolu
Karabük
Soğanlı Çayı
Prusias ad Hypium
Konuralp
Düzce
Eskipazar
Gerede
Bolu
Abant Gölü
K Ö R O Ğ L U D A Ğ I
Sarıyar Barajı
Hasanoğlan
Elmadağ
ANKARA
Gordion
Yassıhüyük
Polatlı
Gavurkalesi
Haymana
Seyitgazi
Sivrihisar
Pessinus
Ballıhisar
Midasşehri
Yazılıkaya
Amorion
Emirdağ
Kulu
EMIR DAĞLARI
CIHANBEYLI YAYLASI
Cihanbeyli
Tuz Gölü
Akşehir Gölü
Çay
Iskali Han
E80
E89
E90
E96

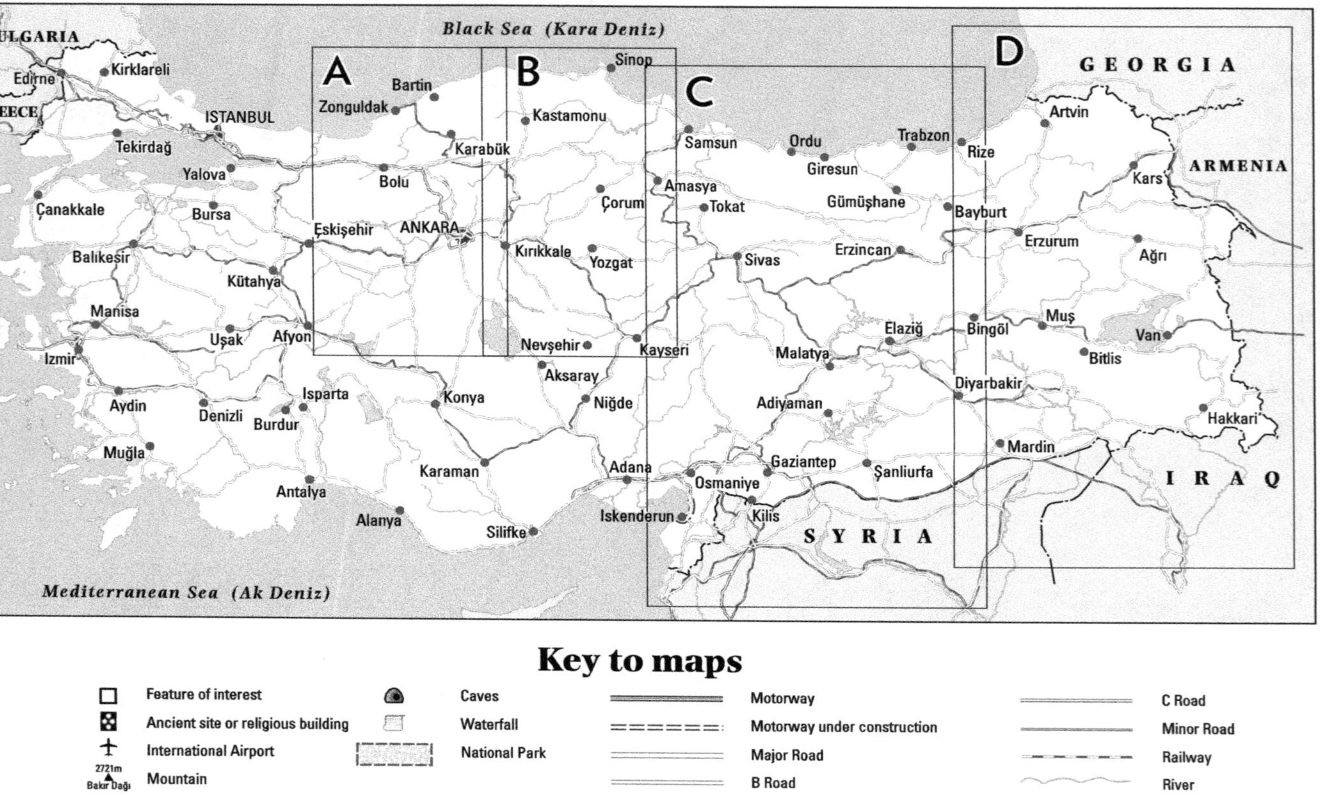
Black Sea (Kara Deniz)
Mediterranean Sea (Ak Deniz)
BULGARIA
GREECE
GEORGIA
ARMENIA
IRAQ
SYRIA
A
B
C
D
Edirne
Kirklareli
Tekirdağ
Çanakkale
ISTANBUL
Yalova
Bursa
Balıkesir
Manisa
Izmir
Aydin
Muğla
Denizli
Uşak
Kütahya
Afyon
Burdur
Isparta
Antalya
Eskişehir
Zonguldak
Bartin
Karabük
Bolu
ANKARA
Kastamonu
Sinop
Çorum
Kırıkkale
Yozgat
Nevşehir
Aksaray
Konya
Karaman
Alanya
Silifke
Niğde
Kayseri
Adana
Iskenderun
Osmaniye
Kilis
Gaziantep
Samsun
Amasya
Tokat
Sivas
Malatya
Adiyaman
Şanliurfa
Ordu
Giresun
Gümüşhane
Erzincan
Elaziğ
Trabzon
Rize
Bayburt
Bingöl
Diyarbakir
Mardin
Artvin
Erzurum
Muş
Bitlis
Kars
Ağrı
Van
Hakkari
Key to maps
Feature of interest
Ancient site or religious building
International Airport
2721m
Bakır Dağı
Mountain
Caves
Waterfall
National Park
Motorway
Motorway under construction
Major Road
B Road
C Road
Minor Road
Railway
River

www.ingramcontent.com/pod-product-compliance
Lightning Source LLC
Chambersburg PA
CBHW060112050426
42448CB00010B/1851